Manitoba

*Directed by Bernard Deforge
and Laurent Acharian*

WHY WE SHOULD TRUST GLOBAL ENTREPRENEURS

XAVIER FONTANET

with Jacques BARRAUX and Gérard BONOS

WHY WE SHOULD TRUST

GLOBAL ENTREPRENEURS

40 years' experience in challenging times

Translated by Rhonda Campbell
revised by Hervé Couvert

PARIS

MANITOBA / LES BELLES LETTRES

2011

www.lesbelleslettres.com

Editor in charge: Laurent Acharian

*To my six grandchildren, their great-grandmother,
my wife, daughters and all those who have helped me become
who I am today.*

TABLE OF CONTENTS

PREFACE: WHY WRITE A BOOK?

A few years ago, in June, Essilor's communications department told me a big weekly newspaper wanted to write about the company. I was a little proud – it's always an honor to receive requests like these. However, I quickly realized that there was no point in replying. Essilor had a good reputation. Why risk it with a negative article? We already gave annual interviews in March and September to the French newspapers *Les Echos* and *Le Figaro* to discuss our yearly results.

I gave a polite but non-committal reply: "Why not write the article later, next year, for example, to talk about the past twelve months?"

"Mr. Fontanet, we'll write the article whether you reply or not," said the journalist, kindly but firmly.

I asked him if I could think about it, and discussed the issue with my team. In my opinion, it was better to give the interview, to avoid misinterpretations and approximations. The team's reactions were mixed. Some were against it, seeing all risk and no benefit for the company. Others were for it, and encouraged me to make an exception and break with tradition. In the end, we decided to go for it.

I called the journalist to tell him the good news. I asked if he would like to visit some of our factories abroad, in the USA or Japan, for example. His answer surprised me: "It's not possible, we don't have the money for that kind of reporting. We'd rather do the article on a French factory." I tried to convince him otherwise: "That doesn't make sense. Today, most of our activity is outside France!"

In the end, we made a compromise. The journalist would come and interview directors during an executive committee meeting. These meetings, bringing together managers from all over the world, are held every month. By chance, the next one was in Paris the following week. While he would be unable to look over the company, he could at least get to know its international directors.

Two months after the interviews, we had still heard nothing from the journalist. We gave him a call. "Actually, Mr. Fontanet, we've thought a lot about it, and we're not going to write the article. Everything is fine at Essilor, there's nothing to write about!"

"Write that everything is fine, then!"

"Noone wants to know!"

I was reminded of a comment a radio presenter once made to me during a commercial break: "You're a nightmare for journalists: there's nothing to criticize at Essilor."

Only in Japan are there detailed articles on the quality monitoring systems put in place to ensure that Japanese bullet trains, run by a private company (a little known fact), arrive within ten seconds of the scheduled arrival time 99.97% of the time.

I protested, reminding him of the efforts we made to get people involved. Joking, I said, "Listen, what will the executive committee think? You stopped us from working, you interviewed most of the directors during the meeting." He saw my point of view, and said he would see what he could do. The article was printed a few weeks later.

It was an excellent article – except for the end. Basically, he said, there was one problem: we were losing market share in France. This is obviously untrue – the journalist confused France's contribution to Essilor's global turnover (which has fallen as the company has internationalized) with our market share in France (which has remained constant over the same period).

In other words, the article needed some criticism, no matter how inaccurate, for it to be published. Did the journalist's colleagues or audience make him feel uncomfortable about writing only good things about us?

This made me think. Papers need bylines to sell. That's what readers want, after all.

When I go to work, when I listen to the radio, it seems as if the world is falling down around us. But when I get to Essilor, I see people doing things, busy, smiling, saying hello. I go to interesting meetings. I wonder whether we're an exception, or whether things are mostly fine and we just talk about the things that aren't.

We need to trust each other, because the world waiting for us outside France is going to change. If we can't build trust between French people, we may not adapt as easily as we will need to.

So I said to myself that to express myself without being interrupted, I should write a book. In a book it is possible to share positive experiences and be read to the end. Of course, debate and even contradictions are essential. No monologue is credible. However, as most information we receive is aggressively split into chunks, I thought going in the opposite direction, telling the full story, would not harm discussion.

This book will also have its blog.[1] I would be very grateful for all of your reactions, and I will reply to your contributions personally. This will allow me to improve any further editions. It's your turn.

Why did I choose Les Belles Lettres as a publisher?

By chance, or by luck (in Chinese, chance and luck are the same word). I met one of the company's vice-chairmen after giving a conference to a group of young entrepreneurs. He lives near me and we spend our holidays in Brittany together, so we know each other. Even though I have a scientific background and I don't write well (or perhaps because of this), I think young people should be taught about literature, language and choosing the right words. I think they should also be taught philosophy – it's one of the best tools for success in the global era they will live in.

Les Belles Lettres have also published some excellent books on economics. In my opinion, we need to rewrite the economics textbooks our children study from. These books are a century out of date. In the chapters that follow, I will outline some ways they could be revised. In my life, chance meetings have played an important role. It's as simple as that!

X.F., Loctudy, August 4, 2010

---

1. www.sionfaisaitconfianceauxentrepreneurs.com.

FOREWORD

I didn't know Xavier Fontanet before working on this book.

Of course, I did know his company, Essilor. I also knew his last name, although it reminded me more of a French Minister than a company chairman. Otherwise, if truth be told, there was no reason our paths should cross.

He therefore called up neither admiration nor antipathy. I was just curious about someone whose values and ideas were, in principle, different from my own.

We got to know each other quickly. We talked a lot. Sometimes we disagreed, because he said things that made me react. I think a lot of readers will do the same.

In the course of our meetings, I came to understand several things.

First, even if he is the chairman of one of France's 40 largest companies, Xavier Fontanet is no different from the rest of us. He is not a man concerned with flashy luxury or unhealthy signs of opulence. Of course, he earns more than other mere mortals. He enjoys certain privileges. But, quite honestly, he is neither imposing nor immoderate.

But that's not all. Fontanet is also a proud liberal thinker, governed by reason. At 60 years of age, he has thought about things. He has used his international experience to test his ideas against reality. His success, or rather that of his company, gives him a real legitimacy. In other words, he knows what he's talking about, yet we don't always hear what he has to say.

During our meetings, I felt like I was hearing something new and valuable. Companies, the market economy and globalization are not the monsters they are made out to be.

To my mind, companies were just entities that sought to make profits. That is what I learned in all my schoolbooks on the subject. Xavier Fontanet thinks otherwise. In his opinion, companies provide services, and profits are merely the reward.

The market economy is not a jungle ruled by the law of natural selection. It is not an ultra-violent environment with no place for the weak. As underlined by Hayek, Schumpeter and especially Bruce Henderson, who all have a place in this book, everyone has a role to play in the economy – as long as we play the game, as long as we specialize, as long as we internationalize, as long as we are continually changing.

In other words, instead of fighting to defend our *acquis sociaux* or social rights (even the term *acquis* is interesting, as it implies French society is completely static), we should be fighting for change, so we can take on the best in the areas we specialize in. Seen from this point of view, the challenge is enticing because we have everything to win.

Here is a man who dares to say that globalization is an opportunity for those who want to get involved. Fontanet's statement is all the more interesting given the crisis currently affecting our economies. Once again, his position is legitimate, because his group has expanded to India, China, the United States and South Korea to become the world leader in ophthalmic optics. He has enough hindsight to see the benefits of internationalization. He also has the wisdom to identify and call attention to the system's excesses, when necessary.

Obviously, Essilor's chairman has thought about what it takes for a French company to succeed in the global economy. But he has not stopped there. He is deeply attached to France. He has a clear view of how France should evolve as a country. His opinion has nothing to do with politics. It is the result of his past experience. It is common sense.

What I like about Xavier Fontanet is how he permanently questions even the most widely accepted ideas. For him, the things that seem obvious, things that people have taught and repeated for years, still deserve discussion.

In some ways, he is a "torpedo" – he wants and needs to get straight to the heart of the issue before accepting or rejecting an idea. As a result, he is always thinking. It's not easy to keep up. His progression is sometimes surprising, but it is always based on his extensive experience.

Finally, the most remarkable thing about this businessman is his honesty. From his point of view, the market economy is a trustworthy system, which has nevertheless led to unacceptable excesses. This has led to a loss of confidence. Fontanet identifies these weaknesses without excusing them. This is rare for a company director.

I thought Fontanet had a tendency to look at the world through rose-colored glasses. I thought his optimism and busy lifestyle prevented him from seeing certain things. It is easy for a company chairman to say globalization encourages upward social mobility. I had the opportunity to talk about this with some of Essilor's employees. I came to the conclusion that Fontanet had not lied. Leaving the company after 43 years service, a trade unionist even wrote, "We must all work towards preserving this great company's human side".

Whether you like this book or not, the important thing is that, after reading it, you will better understand the workings of the market economy. Who knows? Perhaps when you go to work tomorrow, it might make you think about things differently.

Laurent Acharian

INTRODUCTION

It is something we do not hear often enough: large French companies or, more precisely, those that operate in global markets, are holding steady, despite the crisis. This development is a fact, and proof that France is capable of adapting to and taking part in globalization.

However, newspapers, radios and television programs only tell us the bad news. One company is closing down; another is laying off staff. Profits are presented as indecent – although really we should be celebrating the fact that something is going right. Dividends are scorned – although they are actually recycled to help finance new activities. Globalization is presented as the source of all evils, and French people expect the government to protect them. The government accepts this role a little too easily. It is as if we were back in feudal times, when peasants accepted the lord's authority in exchange for protection against the Huns or the Normans.

Globalization is an extraordinary opportunity for society and business alike. Currently, France only accounts for 5% of the world economy. Globalization could allow French companies to become 20 times larger than if they operated solely in France. And it is not just about size. As they come into contact with new methods, processes and cultures, companies and their employees grow and progress. Although companies listed on France's CAC 40 and SBF 120 indexes are often denigrated, they have come an extremely long way in the last 20 years.

France is an attractive country because of its climate, natural landscapes, culture, and people – who think both creatively and theoretically. The country has what it takes to attract multinational companies.

However, its international image has been tarnished by events such as the repeated port strikes in Le Havre and Marseille, and cases of "bossnapping" at companies like Caterpillar in Grenoble. The managers of major multinational companies are not masochists. Why would they want to move here? The repercussions of these events affect the whole country. This is obvious after speaking with the directors of major multinational companies. Everyone – from journalists to trade unionists – must realize they play a role in building the country's international reputation. This book was written with these people in mind.

Globalization forces countries to change some of the ways they do things. Some undergo a complete transformation, while others, like France, are a little more hesitant.

For the last 30 years, the French public sector has stood out for its overzealousness. Its role extends well beyond the traditional realm of state powers. Public spending has increased from 27% of GDP, at President Georges Pompidou's death, to 56% today. This recurring trend has gone hand in hand with budget deficits. Initially, these deficits seemed manageable. However, repeated over 30 years, they have led to a debt amounting to over 80% of GDP.

Today, France is approaching the limits of what is manageable. The Greek crisis was a wake up call: we are walking an extremely fine line. Our taxes are the highest in the world, and lenders are becoming more demanding. The government is finally beginning to realize how sticky the situation is.

The public sector has justified its expansion by claiming to protect against globalization and counterbalance the market economy. In doing so, it implicitly points the finger at all those involved in globalization, especially companies. This is completely paradoxical: companies are probably the best placed to help countries take advantage of the benefits of globalization. Instead, they are made out to be villains.

I know that I am saying things that go against the grain. I may not be understood. However, I spent 20 years at Essilor, first as the CEO, then as chairman. This experience was so useful that I think it is important to share it with you.

I am not naïve. I know life is not a bed of roses. There have been, and always will be, people who do unacceptable things. Nevertheless, I choose to be positive.

Company directors are criticized for not expressing themselves. It is true that we are more about "doing" than about "saying". With this book, I want to tell you about things as I see them.

I will start with the history of Essilor. This will give you an idea of my experiences over the past 20 years.

I will try to demonstrate that companies are not the monsters they are made out to be. Companies are places where we can grow as people and discover... trust.

Trust leads to small miracles. Where there is trust, people are flexible, adaptable and ready to take initiatives. To be flexible, a person must be self-confident, trust others, and trust the system. Companies that foster trust are constantly changing and can anticipate movement. Companies that are ruled by suspicion are rigid and unable to adapt to today's constantly changing world. Trust is probably a company's most important asset. In my opinion, this is also true of countries.

Unfortunately, French people's suspicion is not limited to business. It extends to the entire market economy. This is somewhat understandable, given the distorted way in which it has been presented to them. We therefore need to start by establishing what the market economy is. As I will explain, it is not based on production (as Marx and many others would have it), but trade. Once we realize this, the system becomes much clearer.

Of course, the market economy is affected by distortions. This cannot be denied. My 40 years' experience in international business has made me a realist. Some faults must absolutely be corrected. But no country can exist without the market economy. More precisely, no country stands to gain from protectionism. This would mean watching from the sidelines – being bypassed by growth as the country's international reputation foundered.

Trusting yourself, your colleagues and the system is essential for good working conditions. Trust also works in other ways. It encourages efficiency. People who feel good about themselves are more creative and enterprising. However, to ensure this trust lasts, there must be a good business strategy. If the strategy is weak, the company will not perform well, and trust fades away.

To develop effective business strategies, directors must understand how the economy and competition work. Economics courses explain the economy as it was 150 years ago. In my opinion, they are completely outdated. In particular, they do not teach our young people about the competition facing them in today's world. We need to redefine the basics. To do so, I will ask you to take a journey with me. It will not be without difficulty. You do not have to come along – you can skip the three chapters on the subject. However, if you do join me, I promise you will not regret it.

Finance is the source of the most serious economic breakdowns. Using real examples, I will try to explain why. Part of the problem is pride, and the mistaken belief that time is no longer a factor to be taken into consideration. I will also show you how finance and financial markets are extraordinary tools, if we use them correctly and in good faith.

The public sector cannot just passively observe the transformation in the global economy. It must change, so the private sector remains operational and the country does not suffer. It must also place its trust in companies and make them an integral part of its overall plan.

This means revising industrial strategies, which have become unrealistic as sovereign debt has increased and government support decreased. I will make some suggestions based on my travels around the world over the last 40 years.

France has everything it takes to succeed. Just look at the French companies that have gone global. French people now need to trust themselves and the system. They must rid themselves of their demons. If French people do not believe in French companies, they are ill-prepared for the world waiting for them. This is true for the media and the public sector. Because they operate internationally, companies are best placed to spread the benefits of globalization. If we trust them and trust ourselves, we can do anything!

PART I

COMPANIES:
TODAY'S BIG ADVENTURE

THE HISTORY OF ESSILOR

At this point, it seems relevant to show how companies evolve by taking Essilor as an example. Parts of the Essilor story will also be mentioned throughout the book.

Background

Essilor was created in 1972 with the merger of two SMEs, which had a joint turnover of 30 million euros ($43 million).

The first company was Essel, an eyeglass manufacturer set up in 1849. This workers' cooperative, owned by its employees, had become the French leader in mineral glass lenses. In addition to inventing Nylor frames – where lenses are attached to frames by nylon thread – Essel was known for Varilux lenses, the company's driving force. This lens had been developed ten years before by Bernard Maitenaz, who led the group from 1980 to 1991.

The second company was Silor, a manufacturing subsidiary of Lissac group. It produced Amor frames – which used shock absorbers to protect lenses – and Orma lenses, the first plastic ophthalmic lenses. At the time, most lenses were made of glass – like the glass used in windows. The company was fully owned by Georges Lissac, who was known for his chain of stores launched under the same name.

By the early 1960s, these two French companies had come to the conclusion there was no point in waging a Franco-French war. Raymond-Jules Cottet and Georges Lissac therefore began quietly discussing the future. The aim was to lay plans allowing the business to expand by concentrating on two key products with international patents, Varilux and Orma. Cottet and Lissac were unable to complete negotiations during their lifetimes, but they wisely instructed their successors – Anatole Temkine (Essel) and René Grandperret (Silor) – to continue working in this vein. Discussions took several years, but culminated in 1972. At the time some criticized the decision, saying the companies were about as similar as apples and oranges. This was a somewhat exaggerated viewpoint, but is indicative of the two companies' very different corporate cultures and the doubts the merger raised.

If the companies had not merged, both would probably have lost ground before being bought up by their American or German competitors. At the time, American Optical, Zeiss and Rodenstock were four to five times larger.

Silor and Essel were representative of two different visions of France. Silor was a family business, owned by Lissac. Essel was initially set up as a Proudhon-inspired cooperative in 1849 before becoming a limited partnership where executives controlled capital. However, the cooperative past lived on in corporate culture. The merger respected both companies, and neither took control of the other.

Grandperret and Temkine had completely different personalities. Each year, they alternated for the top spot, providing the teams with an excellent example of cooperation and respect. This positive beginning, where the chairmen led by example, was essential to Essilor's success. It meant that respect and dialogue became an integral part of the corporate culture, and helped the company successfully expand with further joint ventures and acquisitions.

Another innovation was Valoptec, an association grouping employee stockholders, which had been planned prior to the merger. At Essel, executives controlled the capital. At Silor, the Lissac family decided to sell stocks at advantageous prices to management, thus allowing them to join Valoptec along with the Lissac heirs.

Deciding on an appropriate governance strategy is an essential step for all companies. It is also something that the general public pays little attention to, even though it is key to the company's long-term success. To understand Essilor, therefore, you need to understand Valoptec.

The Valoptec charter

Valoptec's charter is one page long. Back then, Essilor's employees were gifted engineers, and literature was not their strong point. This simplicity of expression meant they did not play with words, but used simple concepts understood by all. Like the company's products, these words have withstood the test of time and crossed international borders.

So what did the charter say?

"Valoptec is an association of responsible persons who hold shares in the company, who choose to work together to control their destiny as far as possible by acting through their main activity, the company."

Can more things be said with fewer words?

This is a concise summary of the best things about capitalism: its respect for capital, risk-taking, and the realization that companies (and not governments) are the source of economic prosperity (taking control of our destiny). The charter is also a combination of realism (as far as possible) and socialism's good sides (solidarity in risk-taking). In other words, before earning money, we decide where we are headed – a shared destiny.

The charter also talks about values. The first is trust – respecting people and encouraging dialogue. The second is autonomy, essential to a decentralized company and accompanied by transparency. The next is loving your job. The final value is customer service, which is fundamental to all companies, and requires professional excellence.

Essilor's values have not changed. They are perhaps even more relevant forty years on. They include trust, respect (for people and for dialogue), personal initiative, decentralization and transparency. Essilor could not have been built if employees had not been given responsibilities in exchange for transparency.

Essilor's involvement in a demanding, high-tech industry, and its quest to develop operations on a worldwide scale, make its story extremely relevant. This message is easily understood, from Bangalore to Beijing. Need we say more?

Breaking new ground: Essilor takes on the stock market

Since Valoptec was created, shares and the stock markets have been the group's guide, judge, backer, cement and pride through employee stock ownership. Being listed on the stock market means implicitly accepting to make a profit.

We all know that making money is essential, whether only to invest or become more independent. However, Essilor never set out to "make money". Our focus has always been manufacturing products, providing a service to the 300,000 opticians in our customer network, and expanding globally. Money is just the outcome of this process, a mark of our customers' respect, and a sign to keep on going.

The company is one hundred times larger than it was 37 years ago. Shares that were worth 0.25 euros ($0.36) in 1973 are valued at 49 euros ($71) today. Simply put, sales have increased 110 times, and capitalization has increased 196 times.

As vertiginous as these statistics may sound, they should be put into context. It is all a question of time: a 110-fold increase in sales over 37 years equates to an annual growth rate of 13%; and a 196-fold increase in capitalization equates to an annual increase of 15%. These statistics might point to a good performance, but not an unrealistic one. Other companies have done much better in shorter periods of time.

In reality, Essilor is more a marathon runner than a sprinter. "Slow but steady" is our motto, so we do not burn out before we get to the finish line.

1972-1990

The first years of the merger were made easier by the group's strong growth. Both companies were on a mission to take over the world: through construction of organic lens plants on the Silor side, and prescription laboratories at Essel. The good thing about the merger was that both companies were looking to expand, but in different and complementary market segments. Sales teams were placed under the leadership of Gérard Cottet, who took over as chairman of the group from 1991 to 1996.

Essilor was unknowingly putting into practice advice proffered by Charles de Gaulle: the best way to build Europe is for Europeans to build together outside Europe. In some ways, General de Gaulle's fantasy is Essilor's reality.

To this end, Essel's subsidiaries bought up European importers to create their own subsidiaries. The joint venture with Hoya, set up before the merger, grew steadily, providing an opportunity to work with Japan's manufacturing industry, and a good source of income that financed many new subsidiaries. Essel's teams also went on to plant the Varilux flag in California.

At the same time, Silor opened organic glass plants around the world. The company boldly set up plants in Bataan, Philippines; Chihuahua, Mexico; Manáos in the Amazon Rainforest; St. Petersburg, in the United States.

Both companies had clearly defined roles: Silor worked with organic materials, and Essel was all about design, prescription laboratories and progressive lenses.

As a result of this expansion, Essilor caught up with the major players in the optical industry. It was the world leader in ophthalmic lens sales between 1987 and 1988. However, it lagged behind in the frame, contact lens and intraocular lens implant fields.

1991-1996

In the early 1990s, I was named CEO by Gérard Cottet, who had replaced Bernard Maitenaz. Philippe Alfroid took over the group's financial management.

During these years, specialist groups began to appear. Until then, a "one stop shop" business model – providing everything from lenses to frames and contacts – had been favored by large eyewear companies (including Zeiss, Essilor, Nikon, Bausch & Lomb, and American Optical). Now, new players began to arrive on the scene: Johnson & Johnson in the contact lens field, Alcon in implants, and Sola and Hoya in ophthalmic lenses. These brands showed how specializing was more efficient compared to a multi-product approach.

Essilor was the first generalist eyewear company to see the advantages in specializing. Lenses were our strong point. We were weaker in frames, contact lenses and implants – where Luxottica, Johnson & Johnson and Alcon excelled.

To specialize in lenses, Essilor had to give up nearly 25% of its annual turnover. The operation took around five years. We sold off our implants and contacts. Most of our frames went to the Logo group in exchange for a share in Essilor's capital, which was gradually reduced. We initially kept our Cartier frames, but sold them ten years later.

It was not an easy time. Valoptec gave general management its unwavering support, without which such radical change would not have been possible. Trade unions were both constructive and trust-worthy partners, who understood our strategic decisions. Fortunately, the lens market was expanding rapidly, which meant the company still grew slightly.

During this period, Essilor's only investment was in photochromic plastic lenses. These lenses darken when exposed to sunlight, which makes them "all-in-one": suitable for indoor and outdoor use. The US group PPG Industries – one of the French company Saint Gobain's competitors – had patents in this field, but needed a partner to apply its pigments to plastic lenses. Essilor and PPG had known each other for a long time. When PPG was finalizing CR-39, an essential component of the first organic lenses, the two companies had worked together and created an environment of trust. The Transition joint venture, set up in 1991, built on this solid relationship.

Essilor's alliance with this prestigious group was an opportunity to introduce high-tech ophthalmic products to the market. It was also Essilor's first foray into the US. PPG helped us understand this great country: we are thankful to its presidents, Ray Lebeuf and Chuck Bunch, and its CEO Rick Elias, for choosing to work with us.

1996-2005[1]

After specializing in lenses and paying off its debts in 1995, Essilor expanded rapidly. It was at this time that Philippe Alfroid and I took over the company's top positions, as chief executive officer (CEO) and chief operating officer (COO) respectively.

---

1. Read the glossary entries TEXTILE and OPTICS before continuing.

Essilor's main competitors were no longer big generalist firms (such as Zeiss, American Optical and Rodenstock), but lens specialists such as Hoya in Japan, and Sola in Australia and the US. Both companies were hot on our heels.

Over the next few years, Essilor expanded internationally, with 80% of its investments taking place outside Europe. Around the world, Sola, Hoya and Essilor battled it out on the technical and geographic fronts, in a real-life game of Pac-Man, as noted by one major newspaper.

In 1990, Essilor led Hoya and Sola, but only by a nose. Essilor's major concern was that its competitors were expanding faster than it was. Previously, the company had been held back by using income from lenses to finance frames, contact lenses and implants. Focusing on lenses would help the company expand more rapidly. At least, that was the plan.

The Australian company Sola had headquarters in California. Hoya had built a market of expanding concentric circles in Asia and had begun moving into Europe. Essilor might have been the market leader, but the game was not yet played out.

Sola then made a tactical error. In attempting to become the world leader in semi-finished lenses, Sola overlooked the importance of laboratories. Essilor saw a window of opportunity. We bought up laboratories in the US, Australia and New Zealand – countries where Sola was already well established. Sola never even saw it coming.

Debt-free, Essilor was able to run with the opportunity. Only then did Sola realize its mistake. It began looking for laboratories, but Essilor already had a convincing lead. In business, time is of the essence.

Obviously, buying laboratories in the US was not just a game we were playing against Sola. We also created an incredible company, which is currently the group's largest, thanks to the drop in the Euro. Between 1995 and 1998, our US presence enabled us to move from being a European to a Western company. America has contributed a lot to Essilor: its strength, *joie de vivre*, dynamism, and professionalism.

America has also taught Essilor about the web, insurance, marketing and speed. America showed us how to trust in the future, believe in a better world and pick ourselves up after being knocked down.

We waged a Homeric battle against the mythical American company Johnson & Johnson for seven years. In the mid 1990s, Johnson & Johnson, the world's leading contact lens manufacturer, decided to expand into progressive lenses. It invested unbelievable sums in battling us, but we were able to hold strong and eventually buy them out. During this long and intense combat, I was extremely impressed by Hubert Sagnières, who was later named COO of Essilor.

Essilor's current prosperity is due to this international investment strategy. With bases in both Europe and the US, the group was in an excellent position to move into Asia.

Our battle with Hoya, world leader in Japan and Asia at the time, took place on another front. Hoya and Essilor both considered that it was impossible to separate semi-finished and finished lenses. In Japan, Hoya was a symbol of operating efficiency in the samurai tradition. The battle was fierce and on a global scale.

A little background: as part of our specialization strategy, we had ended our Japanese joint venture with Hoya in 1992, launched by Essel 20 years before. Hoya had been very honorable in their dealings with us. However, they were our competitors everywhere else in the world, especially in the field of progressive lenses. It was difficult to be friend and foe at the same time. We wanted an unambiguous situation. This meant taking a step backwards. Essilor therefore gave up everything it had in Japan (except the brand). We did not regret our choice. It meant we were able to join forces with Nikon to challenge Hoya on its home turf eight years later.

This was not just a strategic move. It meant that, ten years after our joint venture with PPG, we had become a truly worldwide group. Nikon is one of Japan's most prestigious companies, known around the world for its cameras. It is also the world's leading producer of steppers, used in microprocessor manufacturing. These devices are essential for the future of the computer industry. Steppers, especially those produced by Nikon, ensure that today's computers double in power and speed every five years. Like many in Japan, the company is very discreet and led by scientists. Its involvement in this field is therefore a little known fact. Currently, the most important progress is being made in miniaturizing. Light travels at a constant speed. Therefore, the narrower the wavelength, the better we are able to control nanometer-scale devices, and the more powerful and faster microprocessors will be. Nikon is one of the world leaders in this technology, and we are proud to be working with them.

Steppers increase the performance of both microprocessors and software. All the major computer companies (Intel, Samsung and Microsoft) are therefore beating on Nikon's door to find out more about tomorrow's steppers, which are key to tomorrow's microprocessors and software design.

Working closely with groups like these gives you an idea of Japan's incredible strength. Articles claiming Japan is stagnating make me smile. Japan is still very present. Its lead in designing sophisticated electronic components for business or private use is only getting wider.

As was the case when Essilor chose to work with PPG ten years earlier, our joint venture with Nikon allowed us to step up a gear.

Nikon is part of the Mitsubishi group, with whom it is an honor to be associated. Essilor is grateful to Nikon's president, Mr. Yoshida, for entering into Japan's first joint venture with a foreign partner. We are also grateful to Mr. Enya for his role in bringing the project to fruition, and to Mr. Kariya and Mr. Kimara for their continued support. Working on a long-term project with such exceptional partners, who run a company at the forefront of the latest technology, is a unique experience.

Essilor was now fully operational in Japan. We felt like tennis players who had discovered a completely new surface and unfamiliar rivals along with it. This new experience was extremely fulfilling. We learned things we were able to put to use in other markets. Japan gave us a strong foothold in Asia and a new challenge for the future.

Japan is in the middle of what will become the world's most powerful geographic area. South-west Japan is within 600 km of Tokyo, Seoul, Shanghai, Hong Kong and Taipei. In my opinion, this region is quickly becoming the center of the world. Essilor is lucky to be well positioned in each of these countries.

Essilor quickly understood the importance of Hoya's presence in South Korea. We reacted by adopting the same strategy we used in Japan. We set up a joint venture with the ophthalmic branch of Samyung Trading, a family-run conglomerate founded by the Lee family. Essilor Korea was born!

We discovered South Korea's industrial strengths. Koreans are gifted at simplifying things, they are born manufacturers. Their production speed is second to none. Like the Japanese, they pay enormous attention to detail, and they are able to successfully combine tradition and modernity. The country has an extraordinary resilience, and its people are very hard-working. You need to visit to get an idea of what is happening on the ground. Working with South Korea is an exhilarating experience. We are grateful to C. T. Lee and his family for choosing to work with us.

While it is relatively easy for European businesses to work in Europe and North America because of the similar cultures, Essilor decided to join forces with other companies before moving into Asia. Our latest two joint ventures in Japan and South Korea have had a major impact on our competitors and the industry as a whole. We now have access to these countries' R&D and highly skilled workforce. To understand this move, we need to go back in time – to 1993, to be exact.

Essilor was internationalizing, but we were unsure of where to focus on next. China? India? Russia? We lacked the human resources to take on three countries at once. Our first impressions of China and India were that there was a very strong government presence. This is an essential condition for groups like Essilor to expand. People often say businesses prefer a weak public sector. Not true – just try working in a country under these conditions. We therefore launched operations in China in 1993, and in India in 1995. We decided to wait a while before moving into Russia. There are very few companies that invested there so early, so heavily, in such a short period of time. It opened up new horizons for us. Essilor was breaking new ground.

Essilor had begun its forays into the Chinese market in the early 1990s. China had a closed economy at the time. We began by seeking out subcontractors to better understand the country's manufacturing industry. Those who travelled to China early and on a regular basis can attest to the astounding progress that has been made over the last 20 years. The country's industrialization took place so quickly that Essilor plants become unrecognizable from one trip to the next. It was obvious that the statistics were not providing an accurate picture of Chinese industry. This was clear from our visits to the massive industrial areas where Chinese plants filled orders by the world's biggest companies. Further evidence was visible at the ports of Hong Kong and Shanghai, and the freight passing through Singapore.

I do not think any other country in the world has ever equaled China's achievements over the last 20 years in such a short period of time and on such a large scale. The economy was opened up. Residents started traveling. Cities grew exponentially. People got younger, because they had more money to take care of themselves. This progress astounded those of us who were lucky enough to witness it. Today, the focus is on bringing progress to inland areas, where the standard of living is lower than along the coastline and causing many problems. Obviously, China's strength is a source of concern for Westerners. The Chinese know that they must take their impact on us into account if the country is to remain harmonious in the long term. However, they also expect Western nations to make adjustments: China has already made so many itself.

After witnessing China's progress, we were unable to understand how people in France could fear change. We could not comprehend their overcautiousness.

Our foray into India was another success story. Indians have smaller eyes than the Chinese, who are nearsighted. The Chinese market is ideal for factory production, because nearsightedness can be treated with mass-produced stock lenses that require no further treatment. Indians, however, suffer more from hyperopia and presbyopia. The market is therefore characterized by lens finishing laboratories. It is impossible to produce all the different lenses required to correct presbyopia without using a two-step process.

Essilor now has around 30 laboratories in India. We have taken part in many acquisitions and joint ventures. Thanks to its IT industry, India is carving a niche for itself in the world economy. Many Indians have studied and worked in the United States. India has a very strong workforce. Its main manufacturing families are now looking to make a place for themselves on the international stage. They may be a few years behind China, but this delay is negligible in the grand scheme of things. India is an English-speaking country, which is a major advantage.

In 20 or 30 years, there will be three main centers: India, China and the West. With the emergence of these new giants, the differences between Europe and the US will become negligible. South America and Africa will also be forces to be reckoned with, but they will not challenge the top three in the next 20 years.

The battle between Hoya, Essilor and Sola was not only waged on the geographic front. It was also technical. Essilor was stronger in design but, thanks to Japanese industry, Hoya was stronger in lens treatments and coatings. Essilor tried to catch up to Hoya in chemicals, and Hoya did the same in design. Essilor's alliances with Nikon and Samyung Trading upset the equilibrium. Sola could not keep up, and was bought up by Zeiss, which became one of the three leading companies.

As we will see below, this fierce competition was the reason why lenses evolved so quickly in terms of thickness, transparency and precision.

2006-2010

Fortunately, Essilor saw the financial crisis coming.

Our international development meant we were used to working in markets where prices are very low (China and India). The growth of low-cost markets in Europe and the US came as no surprise, as our expansion in Asia was conditional on our activity in these countries.

We knew the financial crisis was coming because, very early on (as early as the summer of 1997), some well-known banks began defaulting on guaranteed investments. Adopting a cautious approach, we launched a major reengineering of the company in early 2008. This helped us deal with the slowdown in October.

Essilor's debts have always been minimal. Our profits and low dividend payouts meant we were able to grow over 10% annually without contracting debts. By slowing organic growth, the crisis helped us to considerably increase our free cash flow. We took advantage of the situation to acquire two world leaders working in industries related to ophthalmic lenses. The first was Satisloh, the leading machine manufacturer; and the second was FGX, the leading manufacturer of non-prescription reading glasses, or readers. Helped by the drop in the euro, the group grew steadily throughout the crisis. What we lost in organic growth, we made up for in growth resulting from acquisitions.

This is the Essilor story so far. The torch has now been passed to Hubert Sagnières and his team, with the full support of the old guard. Hubert knows Essilor well. He helped successfully launch operations in the US and, during the crisis, was invaluable for his work on costs and acquisitions. According to our "meritocratic" system, he fully deserves this role.

I do not know how to thank all my colleagues at Essilor, without whom this would have been impossible. This book is the fruit of my experience. To all my colleagues I am deeply grateful.

Note: In 2009, Essilor had around 40,000 employees worldwide, a turnover of 3.8 billion euros ($5.4 billion) and 11 billion euros ($15.5 billion) capitalization. It had manufacturing operations in over

50 countries. Since 2007, the company has been listed on the CAC 40 alongside much larger companies that are active in bigger markets. The French cooperative of the 19th century has now become a global leader. This "*petite France*", with its traditions and contradictions, set out to take over the world. Its success is due to the men and women working there who chose to believe in growth and globalization. We have no regrets.

A PROFESSION FOR LIFE

"What does my job mean?"

Many employers misinterpret this question, which human resource managers are hearing more and more frequently. Companies encourage their employees to go on humanitarian missions organized by foundations. This is good, but not good enough. It makes young people feel useful and like they are helping others. But their search for meaning goes deeper than this. It is not just about life outside work. Professional life must also have meaning. This is an important message, and not only relevant for young people.

In France, there is a story about three stonemasons who were building the Chartres cathedral during the Middle Ages. The three stonemasons were asked what they were doing. They gave three different answers.

"I'm breaking rocks," said the first man.

"I'm sculpting stone," said the second.

"I'm building the cathedral," said the third.

In other words, it is all about how you see things. Your perception of your role has an impact on the enthusiasm and energy you put into it.

In the story above, the first stonemason is a robot, the second is an artist, and the third is an artist who sees the bigger picture. His personal talent is making history.

Each man uses the same tools and techniques. The difference comes with expertise: the first man does, the second embellishes and the third makes the work his own. My view is that everyone in the workforce is taking part in an epic adventure. They just need to be aware of it.

Auditors are another example. One of their first tasks is to draw up an inventory of a company's assets. Counting the pairs of shoes or bottles of perfume in a deserted warehouse may seem like a thankless task. But in certifying the company's accounts, auditors play a much more important role: they allow us to put our faith in figures, which contributes to the strength of the economy.

The same goes for garbage collectors. They get up every morning at the crack of dawn to pick up our garbage and throw it into a truck – at the risk of personal injury. Garbage collectors play a key role in keeping cities clean, and therefore maintaining our quality of life. By making cities more attractive, they indirectly affect whether big companies decide to set up there. To understand how important garbage collectors are, just talk to the people living in Naples, who recently had to live surrounded by mountains of trash.

Labor

The French word for labor is "*travail*". I only ever use this word carefully. The word itself is not especially positive: it comes from the Latin word *tripalium*, which was a three-staked instrument of torture. Inherent in the word *travail* is drudgery, repetition and the absence of creativity. Charlie Chaplin portrayed this well in *Modern Times*. Labor – on the assembly line in this case – is divided into tasks. Workers do their time and are completely interchangeable. They have no real know-how. Their only aim is to earn money to live. In this situation, living is only done outside work – if the pay is high enough. But with unskilled labor, the pay is rarely high enough. If you do not enjoy what you do, you spend half your life on hold. If you see your profession as "labor", you risk becoming depressed. Essilor has bought companies in the former Soviet empire, where labor was still something you were forced to do. Workers had no real aims for the future. They were just breaking stones.

Profession

I prefer to use the word "*métier*," or profession in English. The word profession means working to produce goods or services that will satisfy customers. The customer therefore plays an important role. A profession is a logical set of tasks, which can be appropriated and improved on. Being a professional requires experience. The longer you stay in a profession, the more you add to it. If you master a profession, you deserve respect. It means you can grow as a person. You also earn better pay, making it easier to become a property owner.

When you are a professional, you take stands and think about things. You innovate and set yourself apart from others. In other words, your labor is worth something, especially because you can pass on your expertise to future generations. Your duty as a professional is to share your knowledge before retiring. This creates bonds between junior and senior employees. Senior employees therefore have a duty to improve their profession before leaving it in the hands of their successors, who will repeat the experience a few years later. This transmission is essential: it generates pride. As time goes on, stonebreakers become stonemasons, even sculptors.

Essilor's experience

When Essel started out as a workers' cooperative back in the 19th century, the profession was relatively simple. However, it quickly became more complex, as machines, chemicals and precision mechanics made their appearance in the optical industry. The profession really gained in prestige when Bernard Maitenaz invented the progressive lens.

The merger between Essel and Silor made Essilor the French market leader in 1973, the European leader in 1980 and the global leader in 1988. Being a market leader has an impact on a company's position with respect to the profession. Being a market leader puts you in a whole new category. The transition is not always easy – you move from being the attacker to the attacked, and your number of challengers increases. Everyone is looking for an opportunity to push you off your pedestal. The biggest challenge is resisting the temptation to become arrogant. It is also difficult keeping up the offensive tactics – in other words, being a leader with a challenger mindset.

At the end of the 1980s, we were only the market leader on paper. To really deserve this title, we needed to expand to other continents.

The first stop was America. Following our acquisitions in the US, we became half American in 1995. This meant half our employees were now based in the US. This represented a major change in culture. It meant that we were no longer just the European market leader, but a Western leader also. We began to be influenced by American culture. We quickly moved on to our next stop: Asia. Today, we have an equal number of employees in America, Europe and Asia.

Imagine what a fabulous experience this was for our workforce. The company was constantly expanding and welcoming new teams. Each year, our plant managers saw their production capacity boom. Our sales teams spent their time travelling to new countries and meeting new clients. Our IT team set up a cutting-edge information system linking 20 key plants and 300 laboratories. Essilor produces over one million lenses daily, many of which require personal monitoring. Our IT requirements are therefore complex. Software designers often tell us that our IT system is one of the most sophisticated they have ever seen. Keeping track of the 80-step production process for hundreds of thousands of lenses produced individually in 300 laboratories is a major challenge. Especially when you take into account the logistics required to get each lens to our 300,000 customers on time.

What an exciting environment for employees!

Essilor is constantly coming up against local and regional leaders in the countries it operates in. While our global expertise is extensive, local companies have better knowledge of the local market. They know how things work; they know all the pitfalls. In tactical terms, knowledge of the local market is priceless.

Learning how to play the game away from your home turf is therefore a real challenge. Multinational companies have this advantage: they know how to adapt quickly by taking into account the local market and adding something new to it.

Working in new countries also means discovering new needs, which can lead to new products. In India and China, for example, progressive lenses are designed to take into account these populations' visual strategies, or ways of looking at things. Thanks to Asia and India, new "ethnic" lenses are on the rise. Essilor decided to look into why myopia develops faster in Chinese children than in children elsewhere in the world. We discovered that it is because they read too closely to the page, which makes their eyes bigger. We are now working with hospitals to develop lenses that slow this process. One day, these lenses will be useful for European children. As this example shows, new challenges encourage creativity. To continually face new challenges, companies must operate globally.

Each country approaches products differently. In Japan and Switzerland, consumers see the machines behind products. This means they focus on instruments, inputs and processes. The Japanese see croissants as an oven, hydrometry, and changes in temperature. So do the Swiss. It is no surprise that Nestlé invented Nespresso – coffee quality depends on machines and improved production processes. Our exchanges with these cultures taught us the importance of machines and production processes, which are a major source of progress. We learned that R&D was not just about lenses, but also the machines themselves. This is why we recently bought up Satisloh, the world leader in optical manufacturing solutions.

Learning all there is to know about a profession is a rewarding experience. Getting to the bottom of things, finding out what there is to know on one subject – no matter how important – is probably better than knowing a little bit about everything. Some are more aware of this than others: universities and scientists are constantly knocking on the doors of world leaders. When you are a world leader, ideas come to you. This is an extraordinary opportunity, as long as you remain curious and modest enough to appreciate others' inventions. A leader attracts knowledge.

To manage these innovations, we had to divide lens manufacturing and sales into 100 different professions. Essilor must be a leader in each one, from chemistry and call centers to complex surfaces.

As far as management is concerned, this makes for an extremely complex and rewarding experience. The profession becomes a real-life experiment where decisions must be made constantly by thousands of people. It is one long learning process for managers.

The lens manufacturing process is a series of many steps. However, it is only ever as strong as its weakest link. Everyone knows this, so everyone strives for excellence.

This might seem insignificant, but it is not. Let us take the example of varnishes, one of our 100 professions. A thin layer of varnish is applied to all of Essilor's lenses to protect them from scratches. We have some of the most sophisticated varnishes in the world. They are applied using extremely complex and efficient machines. A good varnish therefore depends on a combination of chemistry and mechanics. Our varnishes are one of our competitive advantages. They are completely invisible to glasses wearers, but they are the result of priceless expertise.

Varnishes are applied using machines. The machine must block the lens before it can apply the coating. It may sound simple, but how do you immobilize a lens without damaging the varnish, which must be applied uniformly to the whole surface so that the lens can be coated in nano-layers? If an instrument touches the lens, it ruins the varnish. How do you pick up a lens without damaging it? This is no easy task. We have engineers who know the subject like the back of their hand: they are amongst the best in their field. Over the last several decades, they have applied billions of layers of varnish to billions of lenses. When they talk about the clamps used to pick up lenses without damaging them, it is absolutely fascinating. As part of a global company, they have the opportunity to see their inventions used in our production plants worldwide. They recently invented a new clamp, which considerably improved our varnish performance and helped them go down in Essilor's history books by assisting hundreds of millions of people. It is an extremely positive experience. These engineers play a key role in our success and our development. We know it, and so do they.

Is it better to know a little about everything or a lot about one thing? Should we focus on general knowledge or specialist expertise – an encyclopedic approach or being the best in the world in one subject? It is probably better to start out by learning a bit about everything before focusing on one thing. In this respect, global specialization is definitely opening up new opportunities.

In the last 20 years, globalization has been a major source of growth. The secret to Essilor's current success is the fact that, over the last 20 years, we have invested over 80% of our money outside Europe. We got on planes earlier than the others – and everyone at Essilor supported this strategy.

Today, we buy a new company every two weeks in countries on all five continents. We pay top prices for good companies, because we are first and foremost looking for teams. When a company has managed to grow and remain profitable, it is because it has a great team. Human beings are social: they learn through interaction with others. This can have amazing results when people from all over the world work for one big company.

Multinational groups will come into their own in the 21st century. The Essilor team is experiencing the same things as the sculptors of the Chartres cathedral. Employees know that what they do is meaningful. We help people see better – and therefore live better – all around the world.

Our decision to expand on an epic scale was the catalyst for our success. The opportunities this created meant we were continually modifying our organizational structure. Without expanding, without this competitive spirit, without constantly calling into question existing technology, our working environment would be completely different. Key employees would not be who they are today. A competitive spirit is essential to company culture. It is difficult to maintain trust without growth. This is true for companies, and it is probably also true for countries.

This is why companies around the world should focus on one goal: growth. A positive working environment has to be part of a global strategy. It is much easier to internationalize today than it was 20 or 30 years ago. This is why companies must strive for global excellence in their chosen field. Globalization is an incredible opportunity. It means all those who trust in their company and want to take part in an adventure can get involved in international events. Major multinational companies allow normal people like you and I to experience extraordinary things. Whatever your field of expertise, aim to be the best, and nothing but the best! This is the secret to success.

WHO'S THE BOSS?

"Beauguitte, I heard you bought a new car!"

Let me tell you about when, where and to whom this statement was addressed.

Claude Brignon is Essilor's director of worldwide operations, and in charge of around 20 major production plants all over the world. We are a manufacturing group: it is one of our key activities. Claude has spent his working life – all 44 years of it – at Essilor. He started out training at one of our plants. We have worked together for 20 years.

Together, we have made key decisions in the fields of technology, internationalization and organization. The outcomes have been both successful and unsuccessful, allowing us to learn from our mistakes. With so many decisions, some were bound to be wrong. Nevertheless, we have expanded, reduced our costs and improved our processes. In short, we have learned a lot together. Over the same period, we have also seen our colleagues succeed, take on more responsibility and grow as professionals. This is, without question, what gives us the most satisfaction. It would not be exaggerated to speak of our pleasure in watching our teams spread their wings.

The above conversation took place in 1995. After much discussion, Claude and I had both come to the same conclusion: we needed to scale back activity at one of our French plants. Obviously, this was an extremely difficult decision. The plant was symbolic, and decisions like this must never be taken lightly.

This plant specialized in the production of mineral glass lenses, a technique that had become outdated with the arrival on the market of new plastic materials. We had to look reality in the face: sooner or later, we were going to have to drop some production lines by closing plants and retraining employees to laboratory professions.

This was the position we adopted. The next step was breaking the news to the trade unions.

At Essilor, we respect our trade unions. As befits their role, they defend employee rights, but they also understand the company's other responsibilities. We maintain this environment of trust by being as transparent as possible, whether the news is good or bad. Our experience has shown us that it is always better to discuss sensitive subjects as early as possible. This gives us time to plan for change and find better solutions than if we acted hastily.

Given the seriousness of the situation (the plant in question was one of the group's historic centers), we called a meeting of the works council. I decided to attend with Claude.

A works council always has its routine: participants sit so they can be seen and heard, they sign forms and so on. I took advantage of this time to talk to Alain Beauguitte.

Alain Beauguitte was the director of the CGT, one of France's biggest trade unions. "Director" is the right word, because he was a professional, through and through. He could be a tough negotiator – I am using the past tense, because he has since passed away – but he was always honest and acted with integrity.

He was a man of his word, and knew how to manage his teams. I have always had great respect for his convictions and personality, and he contributed to Essilor's success by creating the conditions necessary for meaningful dialogue between employees and management.

Coincidentally, Alain Beauguitte and Claude Brignon started at Essilor on the same day, at the same plant. Both men have had successful careers with us, in very different ways. While they may have had opposing views on some situations, they never forgot their shared beginnings.

The above statement was addressed to Alain Beauguitte at the beginning of the works council. At Essilor, we all call each other by our surnames. The conversation is therefore punctuated by "Beauguitte", "Fontanet" and "Brignon." Beauguitte replied to my comment on his new car by saying, "Fontanet, I have the right to change cars if I want to!"

"Of course you do, but I heard you also changed brands. You bought an X instead of a Y. That's what surprised me!"

"My X broke down. I have the right to punish X by switching to Y, it's a free country!"

"Of course it's a free country. My X is unreliable too, but I still buy the brand. I complain, I tell them what isn't working, but I'm still there."

"Well, I'm not!"

"Beauguitte, do you know what that means for the company? Because of you, labor is moving from X to Y. Have you called your colleagues in X's factory to let them know you're now buying Y? I would have."

By that point, everyone was wondering what my point was.

We started the meeting by dealing with issues that were easily resolved. We then got to the heart of the matter. Before Brignon explained the situation to employees, I intervened again.

"Beauguitte, can I see your glasses? Beauguitte, you're wearing plastic lenses!"

"Fontanet, I have the right to wear whatever I want!"

"Beauguitte, of course you do, freedom is a good thing! But you realize that if even you, as someone who works in a mineral lens plant, buy plastic lenses, Claude has no choice but to cut down or stop production? We're not shutting down the plant, the customer is!"

You can imagine the discussion that followed.

"Beauguitte, seriously, go and see all your friends at the CGT and sell them 10 million glass lenses. Once you have the down payment for their order, come back and see me, and I promise we'll keep the plant open. But without the money, what choice do we have?"

The plant's closure was inevitable. My demonstration had proved it. But by making the announcement ahead of time, we were able to give staff the option of moving to a neighboring plant manufacturing instruments or its prescription laboratory.

For this excellent team, changing profession was not a major issue. The employees had a lot of experience: there was a link between the age of the product and the age of staff at the plant. Some had reached retirement age and chose to leave. The transition was a smooth one.

In our economy, customers are free to buy what they want when they want. In other words, purchasers have flexibility on their side. Why is this not also true for producers? If there are too many restrictions on producers, their bank balance suffers, which in turn eats into their capital. The company's survival is at stake.

Defending jobs in the short-term by forcing companies to keep on staff at whatever cost puts companies at risk of going under. It is not beneficial to employees either, because they eventually have to pick up the pieces.

We need to strike a balance between protecting employees from unemployment on the one hand, and protecting companies that need to reduce production if orders fall on the other. Free trade cannot coexist with overly restrictive regulations. This makes companies suffer, which in turn has an impact on employment.

Employment law (social security contributions and employment contracts), competition law (the maximum market share allowed to producers and distributors) and commercial law all form a single system. In the US, distributors can have large market shares, but producers are given a lot of freedom. In Asia, big distributors are frowned upon: these countries prefer higher sales prices on the domestic market so producers are in a better position to export.

Here are some figures showing how these restrictions affect French companies. When you decide to switch to a new brand of car, you take around 50 hours of work away from the manufacturer. Let's say the company has to reduce staff as a result: it pays two years' wages in redundancy or 50,000 euros ($72,200) to the employees laid off. Fifty hours is equivalent to one thirtieth of the 1,500 hours staff members work per year. Therefore, if consumers played by the same rules as French companies, they would have to pay the company one thirtieth of $72,200 each time they decided to change brands. $2,407! Did you ever think of that?

Ours is a free world. It has advantages but also drawbacks, in the form of uncertainty. We therefore need to be consistent. Some restrictions are worth it. Whenever I visit a country where freedom is not a key value, I see broken people.

Just visit the border between North and South Korea.

It is a fascinating place, where you can see North Korea through binoculars. It is an edifying experience. Especially when you consider that these two countries were one only 60 years ago.

At Essilor, we are lucky enough to have people who understand and support general management. They trust us, and we trust them – to the point that they are completely open with us. This allows us to be flexible, which creates security in this ever-changing world. Essilor cherishes this shared trust.

"MY DAUGHTERS WILL NEVER WORK FACTORY JOBS"

Mrs. Brisson replaced Alain Beauguitte as the CGT representative at Essilor.

One day, she was in an especially good mood. I quickly understood why. Both her daughters, her pride and joy, were studying at university. "Mr. Fontanet, my daughters will never work factory jobs like me."

I replied, "You should thank my predecessors! Your daughters won't have to work factory jobs because Essilor began moving production overseas 32 years ago."

What does that have to do with anything, you might ask.

At the end of the 1970s, five years after the merger, Silor's former employees travelled the world looking for places Essilor could set up production plants. A major plant was built in Florida.

Meanwhile, Hoya, one of our Japanese rivals, had moved its production to Thailand, and was starting to supply its European subsidiaries with lenses made in Asia. Back then, Essilor had no presence in Asia. Because salaries there were 15 times lower than in France, this was a real threat to many of our products.

Thanks to our progressive lens sales, Essilor was growing steadily. We could have chosen to focus on top of the line products. But that is not really our style. We were reluctant to stop any of our production lines, so we decided to move some of them abroad. We opened a plant in the Philippines, and another in Thailand. We had two main objectives: to supply Europe with low cost lenses and set up shop in Asia.

We then had to deal with the public and political outcry. Everyone had something to say, generally along the lines of: "With those profits, Essilor could afford to lose a little on a product line!"

Those who preceded me at the head of the company were right to ignore these comments. Moving production overseas when the company is profitable means you are able to spend what it takes to make sure the operation is a success.

What our critics did not see was the good these plants did in the cities they opened in. Why does this never make the headlines? Not looking beyond our own doorstep is just another form of egocentricity.

People do not travel enough. Our Filipino plant opened in Bataan province, south of Manila. It has been operational for 32 years. It is an integral part of the community. As the cafeteria is comfortable and spacious, it is often used for weddings on weekends. The sports facilities are open outside of work hours. We gave our staff more social protection than was required of us under Filipino law. Our employees have therefore stayed loyal to us and, today, their expertise is close to that of their European counterparts. The plant is one of the most efficient worldwide. This is not surprising given the great volumes of products passing through employees' hands.

Over the years, I have observed employees as they come to work. Initially, they came on foot, then they came by bicycle. Next they came on motorcycles and, today, they come by car. Last year, we celebrated the fact that children of staff at these foreign plants had been accepted to study at US universities. In 30 years, our foreign plants have major impacts on local communities. When employees are treated well, what is the difference between an NGO and our manufacturing plants? Relocating production boosts employment in the host country and improves standards of living in local communities – as long as the company is in it for the long haul and acts ethically.

Another thing the critics fail to see is the distribution centers we were able to set up in Asia thanks to operations at these plants. If Essilor was relatively unscathed by the recent crisis, it is because our business in Asia was booming. This is only possible because we were wise enough and bold enough to set up in this region a long time ago.

If we had not moved production abroad, who knows where Essilor would be today?

In France, if you plan things in advance, you have time to retrain employees who must, of course, be willing to accept change. Having time up your sleeve means you can manage each situation carefully while respecting individuals.

To understand the impact of these operations, we need to look at the bigger picture. The number of people employed by Essilor France has grown 0.5% per year for the last 30 years. However, today's division of labor is completely different. The proportion of unskilled workers employed by Essilor has dropped from 75% to 35%. Most new positions are for engineers, IT specialists, scientists, lawyers, marketing specialists and so on. This is true for France and the other developed countries we operate in.

Training is essential to help employees adapt to situations where production has been relocated. It can be organized if the company plans far ahead enough. Training is also essential for the children of these staff members. The education system must ensure that the children of unskilled workers are able to move up in society and become skilled employees. This is exactly what happened with Mrs. Brisson. It is definitely something to celebrate!

In the end, there are benefits for everyone in relocating production. The new plant's host country gains new jobs, but at the same time the home country gains in social mobility.

There is one condition: there must be a good education system. Today, we are quite rightly identifying the areas where public spending should be cut to reduce the budget deficit. However, it is perfectly clear that these savings must not affect the quality of our schools or universities.

Our education system must compare favorably to those in other countries. This is the only way we can be sure our children will adapt to competitive environments when they are old enough to work. Comparisons between education systems, even if they irritate when we are not highest in the rankings, are absolutely necessary. Our schools and universities must learn to accept them.

Ideally, our schools and universities should be able to open independent and profitable campuses in other countries. It would be proof of their excellence. They should also welcome more foreign students. At big English and American universities, foreigners make up around 20 to 30% of the total student body. This international focus would reassure those of us who entrust universities with what we hold dearest: our children and grandchildren. After all, big American, English and Swiss universities are opening campuses in Asia that seem to be growing quickly. Some of french business schools have also successfully taken up the challenge. For example, Essilor works with the business school ESSEC, which has opened a campus in Asia.

If our education system can take up the "international" challenge, this will create a win-win situation for all those involved. Essilor, a microcosm of the French nation, has successfully proven it over a generation.

ONE BIG, HAPPY FAMILY

Most of our investments between 1995 and 1998 were in the US. From 1998 to 2005, they were in Asia. Since then, we have built solid platforms all around the world, and we invest in countries on all continents, especially India and China.

The companies we work with as a result of acquisitions or joint ventures are involved in extremely high-tech professions. To use their machines, you need mechanical and IT skills; to apply their varnishes, you need to know about chemistry; and to use their vacuum chambers, you need to know how to work in extremely clean environments. The people who join our team are excellent technicians. Customer service is another key aspect of our profession. We deliver to opticians every day at a given time. The profession therefore requires a combination of technical expertise and customer service. Our partners, who have often started at the bottom and built their way up, are real entrepreneurs with both technical and commercial skills.

Every month, two new companies join the Essilor group. We know these companies well, because they are usually long-standing customers. They buy our semi-finished lenses, and we know their directors personally. Our relationships with these companies are not just about money: that is what makes these experiences so rewarding.

Here is an e-mail from Brazil that I received on April 28 as I was writing a chapter of this book. I wrote back straight away. Judge for yourselves.

Dear Mr. Fontanet,

We are pleased to be writing to you as Essilor Group and Optical Laboratory XXX cement their partnership. [...] This union recognizes our professional achievements thus far and our progress in the Brazilian and international markets. [...] We would like to assure you of our continued efforts in research, improving customer service and, consequently, the creation of opportunities for growth in the market. The quality that we would like to associate with our services will be well received at Essilor, a group dedicated to furthering the research and investments that widen our market. Laboratory XXX got off to a modest start 16 years ago, when we sold our car, a Volkswagen, to rent a 130 square foot shop in the city center. We began producing eyewear for the market of the regional capital. With effort, attention and good partnerships, we began selling products with surface technology. Today, we are proud of our experience and determination in building the company.

With our colleagues, we make up a team that is ready to learn, share progress, fight for growth, work together and rejoice in our successes. This is our heritage. Our experience and our credibility reinforce our position to our colleagues. Today, we are convinced our company will have a more prosperous future. Joining Essilor is a privilege and a pleasure. We are committed to our partnership at the head of this new company. [...]

Please accept our best regards as we celebrate this new era.

Yours sincerely,
Adriana

I immediately replied.

Dear Adriana and Luiz,

I was deeply touched by your email. I would like to welcome you and your teams to the Essilor family, and I thank you for choosing to take part in our adventure. You will discover a group of people who are committed to customer service and quality products. I wish you all the best and I hope this new phase of your life brings you much satisfaction on both a personal and professional level.

Yours sincerely,
X. Fontanet

Adriana and Luiz are now part of the Essilor family. They will take part in all our conferences and technical meetings. We will ask them to tell us their story. They will undoubtedly have experiences and original ideas to share with us. At Essilor, they will find solutions to problems they have been unable to solve alone. By joining the group, they will grow stronger. We also gain by taking part in a rewarding experience. A new adventure will begin for them... as one of us.

In Asia, Latin America and India, businesses are seen differently. As financial markets are newer and less developed than in Europe, many companies are still family-owned.

The first time I realized this was in the early 2000s. We were about to enter into a 50/50 partnership agreement in Asia. Generally, when we are finalizing agreements like this, there is some last-minute tension as we discuss the price. But not this time! The owner made a movement as if he was sweeping a pile of cash off the table and said, "I'm rich, you know, I'm not after more money. The price is fair, I don't want to haggle over a few dollars. My real concern is that I'm sharing with you my life's work. I'm entrusting you with what I hold dearest: my employees and my children." We started talking about his teams. He described each one seriously and knowledgeably. He knew them all extremely well. I came to a sudden realization.

Essilor needed to be a family, and this was the vision we needed to have of the group. It was also a natural extension of the Valoptec experience that had not yet been expressed in as many words.

I had another equally important realization three years ago. I was in another country, visiting a company with whom we had signed a partnership agreement three years before. I like these courtesy visits, because they let me see how things are going with our partners and whether they are happy with the joint venture or acquisition. Our partners are our best advertisement: any company that considers joining forces with Essilor always talks to others that have already taken the plunge.

Our partner was an extremely courteous and distinguished man. He took me into his office, closed the door, and said, "Mr. Fontanet, I'm no longer young, I'm entering into the final years of my life, and I'm very happy."

He continued: "I wanted to tell you that I'm happy because my family will stay together after I die. If I hadn't joined forces with

Essilor, I'm not sure the family would be as close as it is now. Thank you for everything."

If globalization has brought about changes in companies, this is surely one of the most important. It also contradicts the things we usually hear.

I often talk about the "Essilor family." Some smile and think I am paternalistic. I know this, but I also know that the Essilor team does not share this view. They know that it is just the best way we have of expressing this feeling of community and entrepreneurial adventure.

In good companies, employees quickly feel what is called *affectio societatis*, meaning they feel at home. They are happy to go to work. Later on, when you become a manager, you are happy to take part in the company's battles and help build corporate culture. You are proud of the company, and ready to defend and protect it when it is threatened or decides to go ahead with a major investment project.

Today, I think the affection people feel for the companies they work in is taking its place alongside affection for family or country. These feelings do not have to be mutually exclusive. It is important that our colleagues have strong family attachments and pride in their country. We need India and China's energy to boost Essilor's performance. This is a harmonious movement.

The positive feelings people have about multinational companies are new, but real and they have strong roots.

I think the 21st century will belong to big global companies. These entities are present worldwide and bring people together. Employees in different countries are able to take part in increasingly meaningful intercontinental exchanges within a single company.

This is why it is inappropriate, in my opinion, to identify big companies as cold-hearted monsters that destroy national identity and cultural specificities. Instead, we should rejoice in the fact that they bring people closer together under one banner. They are the best way to build lasting peace between different populations in today's society.

SHE INSISTED ON PAYING

Manila's shantytown

One afternoon in 1991, I was coming back from Bataan, five hours south of Manila by car, where our first Filipino plant had been set up. The weather was nice, and we got to the airport faster than usual. I was early for my flight, so I asked Jean-Pierre Mazzone – one of Essilor's campaigners who set up plants in Asia – to take me into Manila's shantytown. In the Philippines, Essilor's employees are members of humanitarian organizations, and they know the place well.

Our profession often takes us into these areas. In India, for example, many of the laboratories we buy are in small industrial zones surrounded by slums. In Rio, our offices used to be opposite the *favelas*, and I visited the area with employees. Manila's shantytown is one of the biggest and most impressive that I have seen.

Once you get over your initial shock, you start watching people and trying to understand what they are doing. My most vivid memory is of the women – mothers. Imagine the courage a mother needs to raise children in that kind of environment. With that kind of energy, they could have had wonderful careers at Essilor, I thought.

I have a technique to avoid wasting time when traveling. I read constantly – history, philosophy and economics. I always have around ten books on my bedside table and, when I go away, I take two, three or all ten with me, depending on how long I'm travelling. I get on the plane and open my book – and do not close it again. It helps me while away the endless transfers and avoid wasting time. For me, traveling and reading go hand in hand.

So as soon as I got home from Manila, I bought all the books I could find on slums. One of the most interesting was Hernando de Soto's *The Mystery of Capital*. De Soto is a Peruvian economist, who has spent his life examining slum economies. He is a fervent supporter of market prices. The book describes the informal economies that represent some countries' main source of economic activity. GDP figures for these nations are often inaccurate, because they overlook this black market. *The Mystery of Capital* analyzes these economies by drawing attention to their formal and informal aspects, including housing prices, official and unofficial taxes, and the payment of "key money." One of the most serious issues is the lack of property rights (as land ownership is generally unclear). Consequently, squatters are only able to borrow money at extremely high interest rates, because they have no assets to use as collateral. Establishing property rights and setting up a microcredit system competing with local loan sharks are therefore two key strategies to fight against underdevelopment.

In the course of my reading, I discovered another, much better known book, *The Fortune at the Bottom of the Pyramid*. I gave it to Franck Riboud, president of Danone, for Christmas at a time when we were both interested in the subject. These two books were a real revelation to me.

Summer 2003, André, Pays Bigouden

I was in the Pays Bigouden in France's Finistère region. An uncle, André Pouliquen, was visiting us for a week. He had been a missionary for 53 years in Maroua, 220 miles north of Douala in Cameroon. He was staying with us to take advantage of Brittany's sea air.

Imagine the family dinners, where he told the cousins stories about Africa as they had never imagined it. We all hung on his every word. One night, he took me aside and said, "Xavier, your caravans are a problem." I replied, "André, I don't have a caravan. What are you talking about?"

André was talking about the caravans visiting African villages to supply residents with eyewear sponsored by ophthalmic lens manufacturers. Essilor does support these initiatives. Retired Essilor employees often accompany students on these journeys. It is an extremely worthy cause, and we encourage it.

"Well, the last time a caravan passed through, I had to step in to stop a fight between two old men in the village. Half the village had been given glasses, and the other half had none. So, one old man said to his friend, 'Did you see that pretty woman that just walked by?'

'I saw her go past, but I couldn't see her properly,' replied the second, who was farsighted.

'Well, with my Varilux lenses, I saw her perfectly. She's beautiful! You're really missing out! Do you want to see her?'

'Of course!'

'Well, bring me $100 tomorrow and I'll sell you my glasses.' "

The two old men struck a deal. Except the second man still couldn't see anything because progressive lenses are personalized. So the buyer went to get his machete, and they came to blows. The bloodshed sent people in search of my uncle, the village elder, who tried to patch up the injuries and get the two old men talking again.

"Xavier, you shouldn't give away glasses, you should sell them. If you give them away, people don't take care of them, they sell them."

Far be it from me to say we should never give away anything: generosity is an essential quality in human beings. You should know when to give, but sometimes it is better to sell.

Aravind's head office

Change of scene. We are now at Aravind's head office in Hyderabad, India.

Aravind is an Indian hospital group, which specializes in cataract surgery. Cataracts often occur early in the Indian population.

This family-owned group carries out 300,000 operations per year, in addition to its other activities.

By way of comparison, a total of 200,000 cataract operations take place annually in France.

For the last 20 years, Aravind has supplied free cataract surgery to Indians who are unable to afford it. It balances out this activity by charging wealthier patients, even though the latter also pay an uncommonly low price – an average of $20 per operation. The company grows 15% per year, and does not receive grants.

We wanted to get to know this group, because we were unfamiliar with their profession. Initially, we just wanted to pay them a courtesy visit. They have an extremely positive reputation in India and worldwide. Our hosts welcomed us warmly, they knew we were specialists in ophthalmic optics. At the end of our visit, we were excited, amazed even, and we said as much to the company's founder. They could see our enthusiasm, and because we were sincere, the discussion continued. The conversation turned to our field of expertise: ophthalmic optics, where doctors prescribe corrective lenses in hospital clinics. With no local laboratories, they were unable to prescribe high quality lenses. We asked them why there was no laboratory at the local hospital, and talked about setting one up. That way their customers would have access to sophisticated lenses like Varilux.

"If you want to, we'll give you a hand." It was a done deal.

Fast forward to one year later. By now, we were selling Aravind our lenses – we had a business relationship with them.

"What can we show you this time?" they asked us. "We'd like to know how you look for customers," we replied.

Aravind organized for us to visit their caravans. The group provides local hospitals with caravans that travel to towns and cities of between 10,000 and 50,000 residents. These caravans carry out visual tests to diagnose serious diseases (like glaucoma, for example) and identify patients needing cataract surgery.

Everyone in town knows when one of Aravind's caravans is coming to visit. They line up and wait their turn to go into the examination room. We therefore signed an agreement with Aravind's directors. We told them we wanted to work with people at the bottom of the pyramid, far away from medium-sized cities, and asked them to help us. Our idea was to build a small eyewear shop in a van following the caravan. This mobile shop would sell ophthalmic optics to those waiting to be examined. It was a bit of a risk, but we thought we might get interesting ideas by talking to these new customers.

At the time, we were only present in large and very large Indian cities. We put some of Essilor's employees in the van, and the son of Aravind's founder promised to help us. Our mobile ophthalmic optics shop was an instant success.

Someone from far away standing in line

I was in Paris in December 2004. I received an email from the head of Essilor India, Jayanth. This email[1] contained another email … sent by Aravind's caravan (an excellent illustration of the efficiency of horizontal organizational structures).

"Photograph of the first patient. She came from very far away but she refused to accept a free pair of glasses. She insisted on paying." (The glasses cost $10)

Her reasoning? "Do you want to destroy my dignity?"

"Gives us some idea about the profile of the rural customer."

It was touching to see this old woman receive her first pair of glasses. Traveling to the city to get these glasses had cost her a fortune. She lived in a small village with a population of 2,000 people where she earned $1.00 per day. She had traveled to the city with a member of her family because, in India, tradition dictates that you never travel alone. Taking into account the three days of work she and her companion missed plus the bus fare, her glasses cost her a total of $20.00, or 20 days work.

We spoke with her and asked if we could visit her village.

When we got there, we discovered an interesting setup in the form of a traveling salesman. This man's business was visiting villages with suitcases of glasses. He appeared on a regular basis to rent his ware to the villagers. We arranged for our next visit to coincide with his.

When he arrived, he was surrounded by village residents, who chose a pair of glasses that more or less did the job. The women threaded their needles, the men read the newspaper. We asked how much he charged for his services. "One rupee every 15 minutes" (a rupee is worth $0.02).

In other words, people pay $1.00 per year to be able to see properly for 15 minutes per week. This is the market: this is what we have to build on.

I will spare you all our failed attempts. However, one of our good ideas was to recreate a medieval fair. The method was very simple. We paid the local council to seek out potential customers for us. We

---

1. See Appendices, T 1.

fixed the price of the glasses at $5.00, dividing by four the price paid by the old woman who refused our gift. As soon as there were enough people on the list, the mayor called the caravan.

When the caravan arrived with its "optician van", people underwent a series of visual tests, including refraction tests. Then, they took their prescriptions to the van. Like at normal opticians, they chose their frames and waited while the appropriate stock lenses were fitted.

With 120 customers per village, $5.00 per pair of glasses and 150 villages per year, this is a profitable activity. Because it is profitable, it is lasting, and will grow naturally. We have been using this model for the last four years. Today, we have four caravans and are preparing a fifth.

What is the next step? It is difficult to say.

Seeking out 120 customers per village is a difficult rhythm to maintain in the long-term. It is also difficult for our teams. Fortunately, the villagers quickly wanted better lenses, and better frames. They were ready to pay more to see well, and women wanted to have different frames from their neighbors. This upgrading compensated for the lower volumes – which says a lot about the profession and its potential. With our distribution model, a pair of ophthalmic prescription glasses costs one week of work, not a month!

When we share this experience, our listeners have mixed reactions. Many say, "It's disgusting. If you can make glasses for $5.00 a pair, your margins in France must be astronomical."

I always answer the question politely, but I am shocked by how suspicious people are about companies, and how little they know about economics.

The price difference comes from France and India's different costs of living. The price of a pair of glasses is 80% locally determined: the optician is local and the laboratory is local. Only the semi-finished lens is not produced locally. The cost of living in France is 60 euros ($85) per person per day, 85 times higher than in India. The price of our lenses in India therefore respects this ratio. As mentioned above, a pair of ophthalmic glasses represents approximately one week of work: $5 in India, and 300 euros ($425) in France for standard lenses. Let me stress that $5 is the price for a standard pair of glasses, not a progressive pair.

Essilor, in order to cater to the poor, has adapted its prices to the local market. Essilor has put the industry's technology at the factor cost of those living in the Indian countryside. This is an excellent illustration of the advantages of globalization. Can you blame us?

Essilor and its teams arrived naturally at this conclusion. No manager ever said, "I want the group to get involved in charitable activities." The suggestion came from our Indian teams, who are reluctant to speak about the experience for fear that these customers will be exploited. Today, we share this experience within the group. A similar experiment is underway in Chinese schools to diagnose visual difficulties in children. The rural marketing model is ineffective in China because the roads are better, so peasants can access medium-sized cities much more easily. Our teams therefore chose another strategy: as soon as the director of a school has 100 children with badly treated eye problems, he or she calls the Essilor bus.

We are currently testing the profitability of this model. If it is sustainable, we will roll it out elsewhere.[2]

Labor, profession, leadership... benefactor?

As we have seen, companies pass through several stages: the labor phase, the professional phase and the global leadership phase. When the company reaches the leadership level, it naturally sees that it is best placed to help the underprivileged because it is present everywhere. Essilor, for example, has at least 500 million customers. We are everywhere, absolutely everywhere, in the world. Whenever someone in the group comes up with a good idea, it can be immediately implemented in the entire organization. Whenever we set up a prescription laboratory in a medium-sized city, this attracts opticians and groups of opticians who see their profitability increase to the point they can open shops. This has an immediate effect on their working conditions, children get better results at school, and self-employed craftsmen work longer. We

---

2. When I talk about our rural marketing activity in India at conferences in France, a lot of young people often come and ask me if they can help. Obviously, it is difficult for them to get involved, because the cost of their air travel almost immediately makes the operation unprofitable. I therefore tell them that there are probably many opportunities to help those at the bottom of the pyramid right on their doorstep; they just need to look. In my opinion, the Adie organization, set up by Maria Nowak, is one of the best initiatives launched in the last 20 years.

have a major impact on local development: this is obvious by visiting sites and opening your eyes.

Correctly run, our daily operations are probably just as effective as community initiatives. This is true in India and in France. Could the key to sustainable development be at the end of the day... the market economy?

BUILDING TRUST

Most people spend a lot of time at work. Generally, this is about triple the time they spent at school. It is therefore a serious problem when people do not succeed at work. Sure, life might be elsewhere, but what a waste of time! Companies should at least allow employees to learn professions. They should also encourage personal progress and development. For this to be possible, an environment of trust is essential.

Rules do not inspire trust; trust is built by actions repeated over time. Trust is difficult to define, but is above all an atmosphere that is absolutely necessary for a company's expansion and success. In turn, success builds trust – leading to a virtuous circle.

Having employees that want to come to work every day is an ambitious goal. Employees should be happy to give their best, and feel that they are making progress. For this, they need to trust their colleagues, management and the company's overarching objectives.

Building and maintaining trust is a mysterious exercise. However, some simple organizational processes and behavior can help.

Organizational processes

My 40 years' experience in business has taught me a simple lesson. When employees are given carefully defined responsibilities relevant to their position in the company, they progress.

Seeing team members grow with and as part of the company is one of the greatest memories I have of my professional life.

For employees to progress, the organizational structure must give as much responsibility to as many people as possible.

Horizontal organizational structures are ideal. Each manager is given responsibility for as many employees as possible: 12 instead of six or seven. This minimizes bureaucracy, increases career opportunities as people take on more responsibility, and reduces the levels of management. At Essilor, each manager is responsible for 12 people. This means that there are only six levels separating the CEO from staff in European laboratories.

When you live in a house with just six floors, everyone is able to interact with each other on a daily basis. This is an essential way of bringing people together in businesses, and in society. When France's elite moved to Versailles, they isolated themselves from the French people. This could explain why the people overthrew the king a hundred years later.

Managers must also learn how to set fair and intelligent targets. Targets depend on the employee's position in the company: sales representatives have weekly sales targets by sector; sales directors have monthly sales targets by region; commercial directors have market share targets; directors of business units have three-yearly growth targets; and the CEO is evaluated in line with value created over a five-year period. Everyone should have targets, whether they are executives or not.

However, targets for form are insufficient. The content must also be appropriate. Deciding on appropriate targets is only possible with regular face-to-face meetings between staff members and their superiors. In these conditions, giving responsibility to employees has positive results. Targets must be appropriate and well thought out: not too high and not too low. Otherwise, targets create internal politics and games that always end badly. The regular meetings encouraged at Essilor have the advantage of building close relationships between managers and their teams.

Finally, for this system to work, performance reviews must be fair. Nothing is worse than unfair managers or mafia-like behavior ("I'll protect you if you don't meet your targets – but only so long as you support me"). These stratagems quickly destroy trust and undermine organizations.

Good target systems therefore require a lot of thought, transparency and care. They are built over the long-term and delve into details. They are a combination of short-term focus and long-term vision.

When employees accept targets they know they will be judged fairly on, a virtuous circle begins. If they meet their targets, this obviously builds trust. Even more interestingly, the system also helps those who do not meet their targets, by allowing them to move beyond their failures. Indeed, failures are often more instructive than successes, if you take the time to analyze them.

I believe that good managers must also have had their fair share of failures, otherwise they risk not being able to learn. This is often a problem with people who have succeeded in their studies – some bad grades would have done them good! In a fair system, you learn as much from your successes as your failures – which are statistically inevitable. Giving individuals responsibility makes them grow.

When an employee racks up repeated failures, I always like to know who appointed them. Often, the error comes from promoting someone too quickly or appointing them to a position they were not suited to. This is important to remember. Employees should know that their boss also has a boss, and even CEOs are responsible for their actions. At Essilor, there is no shame in admitting your mistakes, and that is true for everyone. It is a form of fairness that helps promote humility.

Performance measurement systems can be used to determine pay issues. Positions are remunerated at the market salary, good performance is rewarded by bonuses, and promotions – based on objectively evaluated performance – are recognized by pay raises.

This system of giving responsibility, determining salaries and promoting employees based on an objective evaluation of their performance is the basis of the meritocratic system encouraged by Essilor. Promotion based on performance is a key value, which encourages an environment where internal politics are virtually absent. It also allows talented new employees to successfully integrate the company, because our profession depends on utilizing new technologies. These highly qualified recruits know Essilor is a "meritocracy." They know they will be treated fairly without having to endure hazing. They also know that their qualification means nothing without hard work in the meritocratic system.

One day, a recruit from one of France's top schools (the École normale supérieure) talked to me about his boss, who was much less qualified than he was. In fact, the manager in question had barely studied at all, but he was extremely intelligent and competent. The recruit said to me, "Mr. Fontanet, I have never had a better teacher in all my life."

Meritocracy works and, when run fairly, is accepted by all.

These are the processes that can be used to build trust, inspire progress and encourage performance-based rewards. We consider they are essential to help foster human capital. However, these processes are not sufficient in themselves, because there will always be untrustworthy people. But they do help.

Behavior

In addition to processes, behavior can inspire trust. It is more subjective, and therefore more difficult to describe. However, positive behavior is always easy to identify.

Respect individuals and foster talent

To respect individuals, managers must respect their work and ideas. Unfortunately, some managers tend to take credit for their colleagues' work or ideas. Fortunately, news always gets out. However, this destroys the team and its creativity. Why go the extra mile if someone else is going to take all the glory?

Respecting individuals is also about getting to know them and taking a real interest in who they are – finding out what you can do for them, rather than what they can do for you. People who "manipulate" others at work are to be avoided.

Individuals are not a set of different parts, but a whole. You cannot separate employees from their home lives. When people have real problems, they are often both personal and professional. You must be able to listen. This means respecting the person, who wants to know you are not faking it.

We all have unique talents (or "genius") allowing us to succeed in different fields. Good companies know how to identify these talents and create environments that nurture them. There are as many talents as there are people. Harmonious workplaces develop when individuals understand they are different to others, and that they have unique contributions to make. However, they must also understand that they depend on others, because no one can do everything.

Listen to others

Some people hear; others listen. Listening means really paying attention. It means understanding other people, and feeling real empathy with them. It is a rewarding experience. It is impossible to make the right decisions if you skip this essential step. Those who know how can help people grow just by listening and asking the right questions. Sometimes another point of view makes all the difference.

Listening to customers is essential to understanding their expectations and anticipating their needs. At the end of the day, they make the decisions, so their opinions are important. The best sales representatives are not smooth talkers, but those who best understand their customers.

Unfortunately, not everyone really listens; many just lend an ear. Some people have too many problems of their own to be able to listen well. Others talk so much they silence anyone else who might want to speak up. These people are major liabilities for companies and, personally, I have little time for them.

Tell the truth

At Essilor, our word is gold. In the past, we have honored erroneous promises made by sales representatives several times. This cost us a lot of money, but it was also a way of showing that making promises is a serious business. At Essilor, everyone knows we honor our commitments.

Many managers do not dare raise issues for fear of angering others. A good boss knows when to say when things are going well, but also when things are going badly. Telling the truth helps individuals and companies progress. It takes courage, but fair managers must know when to speak up. Misunderstandings are like time bombs – they will eventually blow up.

Give responsibility

The flatter the organizational structure, the more efficient the company. As I have said, a good director must be able to lead up to 12 good managers. Unlike pyramid structures, horizontal organizations have the advantage of encouraging the circulation of information (and preventing disinformation).

Horizontal organizational structures require competent employees who understand quickly and interact efficiently. Vertical structures create middle managers and infighting – too many people with not enough to do. Even worse, this generates bureaucracy. Responsibility helps people grow, but bureaucracy is a barrier to progress.

Get external advice

I am suspicious of bureaucracy, and I can tell you that it is not limited to the public sector. It might be suited to some organizations, but it is not appropriate in businesses that must remain competitive.

Consultants are the perfect addition to horizontal organizational structures. Consultants know things you do not. Thanks to their experience in other fields, they can provide you with new perspectives, tell you how you stack up against your competition, and advise you on how to improve. At the beginning of my career, I was a consultant. I therefore appreciate their abilities. Good consultants make valuable contributions to companies – when they have been chosen well, when their objectives have been well defined and when they are leaders or future leaders in their field.

Be transparent

Give everyone the same information. I dislike speaking with people who are in a weaker position because they lack information (just as I dislike being in a weaker position because I have not been told the whole story). It is a question of dignity.

Our trade unions are given the same information as the executive committee and financial markets. This transparency is because of our history, but also because we are convinced people react better to situations when they know what is happening. Transparency is necessary before you can give teams responsibility. It means everyone is moving in the same direction.

Manage fairly

Not rewarding employees who meet their targets is as unfair as rewarding someone who has not. Unfairness often takes the form of favors, and creates inequalities in the workplace. This leads to an unhealthy environment where employees have no incentive to perform their best.

During the French Revolution, the *sans-culottes* saw happiness as being dependent on equality. In management terms, there is nothing more unsatisfactory than average. Imagine if a teacher gave the same grade to all the students in a class. It discourages good students from working, and encourages bad students to keep up their bad habits. Being courageous enough to recognize differences in performance is one way of granting justice, and essential to healthy businesses.

I see the same situation all around the world: fair managers create good working environments where good practices are adopted; and politically minded managers create environments where bad practices (doing the minimum) are adopted. In this respect, things go quickly downhill.

Celebrate

At Essilor, we celebrate our successes. Whether it is because the group won a contract, an expat returned from abroad, a new product was successfully launched, a staff member won national recognition or an employee won a long service award, we celebrate. These celebrations have many advantages. As social events, they help build team spirit. They also show team members how important they are to the group. As we have seen, a company is a family. When one of your children graduates, you crack open the champagne. Why not do the same for your colleagues?

Be confident

To perform well, you have to respect others, but also yourself. Team members should have confidence in their skills and qualities. The manager's role is to help them assert themselves and give them the energy they need to move forward.

However, there can be too much of a good thing. Self-confidence can become arrogance, with catastrophic results. Both feelings are linked. Arrogance is the risk run by the leader. I often say that humility should grow faster than market share.

I mistrust people who are too sure of themselves – whatever their age. From experience, I know the most brilliant experts are often the most humble. The best way of fighting arrogance is by competing with other companies and regularly visiting customers.

Accept change

When I look back on my 20 years in an operational role at Essilor, I realize that there were major changes every year – in production, engineering, purchasing, organization, stockholders and activities. Change became a habit.

We had to change constantly, because our environment was changing. The key is anticipating change and not hesitating in your course of action.

Changes should be seen as new opportunities. You should accept to learn a new profession, experience life overseas, and share your expertise on another site. Companies need this flexibility to expand.

Change brings growth, and growth helps everyone move forward. I would not know how to run a company without growth.

Aim high

Trust is created by setting targets and attaining them. Becoming number one and staying there is an adventure all employees want to experience. It means their actions and daily routines take on historical proportions. Everyone contributes in their own way to a project that becomes more than just the sum of its parts. Trust means trusting yourself, others and the system.

Obviously, a good working environment depends on a good strategy. Management and strategy go hand in hand. They either work together or cancel each other out – both are necessary.

Hire CEOs internally

Trust is built in the long term, and must be won daily. CEOs only earn their employees' trust after a few years – around five, I would say. Employees watch what CEOs do and the positions they adopt on different subjects before giving them support. CEOs must therefore stay in position longer than five years, because otherwise things will stop when they should be getting started.

The idea that CEOs have power is false – the power is actually in the customer's hands. The CEO serves the community he or she leads, and for which he or she is responsible.

Being a CEO is not about the money. CEOs should be hired internally – to consecrate the "meritocracy." CEOs must link the worlds inside and outside the company, by inspiring trust on both sides. Some situations may justify hiring a CEO from outside the company, but this should be the exception rather than the rule.

PART II

THE MARKET ECONOMY AND ETHICS

THE FIRST SALE

His first sale

It was ten years ago and we were spending a weekend in Normandy, where we had a house. I was wandering through a market on the square outside the bakery when, at one stall, I saw a small wooden bench that looked new. I looked closely at it. It was exactly what I had been looking for – something my grandchildren could sit on by the fire. I had looked through several furniture catalogues in vain, and here was the answer to my problem.

I approached the stall to find out more. A shy young man greeted me, and we began talking. I realized that he was the one who had designed and built the bench. He had begun working at the family business, and it was his first piece of furniture. The workmanship was remarkable, and the bench perfectly proportioned. The young man had obviously inherited the Norman carpentry skills, because the varnish was perfectly applied. It was a very nice piece of work. It cost 25 euros ($35).

I said to the young man, "I'll take it for 30 euros" ($42).

He took my money wordlessly. He did not know what to say, or what to do with the bills in his hand. I encouraged him, "It's your first piece of furniture, and it's beautiful. You're an excellent carpenter – if you work hard, you'll go far."

I will never forget the smile he gave me, nor the way his eyes lit up. I have always thought that, in buying his bench, I did him more good than I could ever have done by simply giving him money for nothing.

The early days at BCG

This story dates back to the 1970s. I had just accepted a position at the Boston Consulting Group (BCG) after graduating from Paris' École des Ponts engineering school and Boston's Massachusetts Institute of Technology (MIT). The recruitment process had been eventful. In those days it was a lot easier to find a job, and young people had more choice. I had had several offers from big French banking and manufacturing firms. The directors were often family friends. When I introduced myself, I was asked questions about my studies but, surprisingly, people were relatively uninterested in the MIT diploma I had just obtained.

I also had job offers from US consulting agencies. When I asked friends and family for their advice, their answer was always: "Be careful of consulting agencies – you'll have fun for a couple of years but after that you'll be unemployable. Start in manufacturing. We know people, and it's better to be safe than sorry."

But one thing bothered me. The salaries offered by American consulting agencies were two to three times higher than those at French companies. Eventually, I gave in and accepted an offer to run a small plant belonging to a French manufacturing company. I was not particularly thrilled by this decision, but it was wise in the eyes of my friends and family. I was a little bitter about bowing to tradition. That evening, I talked to a good friend, François, who said, "Xavier, you're making a monumental mistake. Before you decide, go and see the Boston Consulting Group. Meet Bruce, who's in Paris tomorrow, and make up your mind afterwards." Bruce was the mythical Bruce Henderson, founder of the BCG.

Bruce was supposed to meet a prospective customer for lunch, but his meeting had been cancelled. To my astonishment, I therefore found myself eating with this living legend.

Bruce was the son of a Baptist preacher, and had spent his youth selling bibles with his father. He had something of the missionary about him as he was very softly spoken. I later understood that this was on purpose, to make people listen to him. He enjoyed discussing economics with me, as I defended ideas I had just learned at MIT, but that (unbeknownst to me) BCG had already moved beyond. We were having a rather heated discussion about price theory when, with a majestic gesture, he spilled his soup in his lap. Without missing a beat, he mopped up the soup with a napkin and kept talking, as if nothing had ever happened.

My decision to join BCG was that simple. In the hour following our lunch, I resigned from the position with the manufacturing group I had accepted only the day before. If the boss of a company was ready to take an interest in someone fresh out of school, have lunch with me and talk with so much passion as to forget the soup he spilled in his lap, he was someone worth knowing!

BCG Paris was a small start-up. There were ten employees, the oldest of whom was 35. We gave strategic advice, a profession that generally requires experience. We compensated for our youth by using tools that were ahead of their time: the experience curve, product portfolio, sustainable growth formula and segmentation, amongst others. In Paris, the success stories just kept multiplying.

Three years and two moves later, the forty-member team took up residence at the former Fiat tower in Paris' La Défense business district. We had taken the French strategic consulting market by storm. The grogginess of the market leaders only increased our determination.

My first sale

I was promoted to manager. I understood the profession, and I was able to manage teams working on small-scale projects. However, I was not authorized to sell our services. Sales were reserved for the group's vice-presidents, who were the only people able to make offers. When a customer requested our help, one of the vice-presidents visited them to learn more about their needs and suggest relevant services.

When these customers then accepted our offers, the vice-presidents created teams of consultants and managers. To put it plainly, the vice-presidents had the power, and they got it from making sales. Only a global committee could promote managers to vice-president positions.

I was a manager, and I could not make sales, but I did have direct contact with customers.

"How much would it cost me, Mr. Fontanet?"

At MIT, computers had fascinated me. In those early days, PCs and spreadsheet programs were still in their infancy. The basic computer was an Apple. The spreadsheet concept, widespread today, was invented in Boston. At the time, the main spreadsheet program was Visicalc, an ancestor of Excel today. I thought this software was fantastic, and I had a real advantage over my colleagues when it came to using it. I had even developed a mathematical model calculating a company's mid-term business plan by taking into account competitors. Basically, it was a model of Bruce's theories. Simply put, I compared the profits and market shares of different competitors in a sector. Each player was a competitor, and the model calculated the effects of different decisions on companies. It turned the uninspiring exercise of the mid-term plan into a real-life game of Monopoly or Risk. My Visicalc calculated the results in seconds, which made the exercise extremely dynamic. I discreetly showed my product to the customers I thought it might interest. There were other models on the market, but none of them had my product's competitive focus or its entertaining approach. They were therefore much less attractive.

One evening, while I was working on a project at Telemecanique, a group later taken over by Schneider Electric, I was called into the president's office. I thought it was because he was happy with my work and wanted to offer me a position with the group.

"Mr. Fontanet, I've been told you've developed an interesting product, I'd like to buy it from you."

I was taken completely by surprise, but I recovered my wits. I wanted to sell it to him, but I was not allowed to. I told him I would get back to him as soon as I could.

I immediately called the head of BCG's Paris office, John Barnes. Fortunately, he was in charge of the Telemecanique account. John was a literary person, and math was not his strong point. Our discussion was short and to the point. He basically said, "Xavier, I have no idea what your model does, but it doesn't matter – I trust you not to do anything stupid. Telemecanique is a big client, one of our biggest. Our reputation in Paris depends on how happy they are with our team. You understand the situation, do your best!"

John trusted me!

The next day, I talked to Telemecanique's president and gave him my price: 180,000 Francs. He said to me, "Mr. Fontanet, I'm very interested. I want to be involved in your work, not just the final presentation. I want to see a progress report every week."

I remember exactly how I felt at that moment: "You trust me, you're willing to take risks – I'll make sure you won't regret it. I'm going to work so hard I'll meet your expectations ten times over."

This experience taught me something important about the market economy: it depends on both parties trusting one another. No sale can take place without it.

Marx's strange view of men

Another lesson I learned that day is that sales precede production. The economy is built around trade. All French people should have to work in sales at some point in their lives. One of the problems in France is that too few people realize their salaries are paid by sales. Too much importance is given to the public sector and the resulting transfers of wealth. In France, the public sector puts food on too many tables. This is no doubt one of the reasons why the French are suspicious of the market economy.

Sales are the result of two freedoms. First, people are free to buy any product they want. Secondly, people are free to sell any product they want. Sales are an exhilarating experience, and some of my best professional memories.

Before a sale takes place, each party makes a judgment and takes on responsibilities (the seller judges the buyer's ability to pay, and the buyer judges whether the good or service is satisfactory). The transaction takes place when both buyer and seller trust each other.

Trade allows people to use and develop their judgment (after the good or service is put to the test). Being able to exercise judgment is part of human dignity. Depriving people of the market slows their personal development. Those who think salespeople manipulate their customers are generally theorists who have never sold anything themselves. Manipulation is key to Marxist theory: capitalists invent machines, produce goods, manipulate customers through advertising and exploit employees – profits result from this power struggle.

The people who hold these views – numerous in France – have obviously never been salespeople themselves.

If they had, they would know that selling is not easy, and there is an art to making a profit through sales. Practically speaking, manipulation is impossible when there is so much competition. Customers are intelligent, and they are increasingly well informed. Thinking that sellers manipulate buyers is also insulting to the latter, because it insinuates they are unable to come to well-founded conclusions. It is a strange way of looking at humanity.

Sales, sustainable development and the public interest

Good salespeople always take their customers' interests into account. Good salespeople think of today, but also tomorrow. Sales are long-term commitments. The first sale is often followed by a second, then a third. Customer loyalty is often one of a good salesperson's main concerns. Loyal customers are the best advertisement for new sales – they create growth.

When sales are repeated, the parties enter into a new kind of relationship: a partnership. Perhaps this is what sustainable development is all about.

In these situations, the individual interests of the buyer and seller converge, creating a relationship that is in the public interest. The public interest may well be served by the marketplace: when consumers are free to act as they wish, companies must continually work to ensure they keep their customers.

Because he was interested in my product, Telemecanique's president sent me an even stronger message: "Xavier, you're good at what you do, your product is innovative, I trust you." By trusting me, he gave me self-confidence and let me be myself. How can you be disappointed in this situation? It was one of the best days of my life.

Leaders that depend on each other

Trade's impact on society often goes unnoticed. Nevertheless, it is because of trade that we no longer need to be self-sufficient: we understand that we no longer have to produce everything, we accept our dependency on others and we choose an area to specialize in ourselves.

How do you choose what to specialize in? The answer is both natural and logical: in the fields in which you have a real talent. Sales are about much more than just trade, they also involve the organization of society.

When you need an electrician, you generally avoid the advertisements of people claiming to provide "electrician–locksmith–household services." Advertisements for "electricians with 25 years' experience" are much more reassuring. It is difficult to be good at everything. I do not believe in being an expert in many fields, or having encyclopedic knowledge. Being average is unsatisfactory for both buyers and sellers. Buyers will not obtain the quality they require and sellers will obtain lower prices than experts. This is true whether you are a craftsman or a big company. Whether you are self-employed, an SME or a big multinationals, competition gives you incentives to focus your efforts on the fields in which you excel.

In the end, trade and specialization should make us all leaders that depend on each another.

SATO-SAN, MY DEAREST ENEMY

In November 2005, I got a telephone call. It was from Sato-san, the president of Hoya Vision Care, the second largest company on the ophthalmic optics market.

"Mr. Fontanet, I have something important to tell you. Could we have dinner together when you're in Tokyo in December?" He knew I would be in Asia for our Nikon Essilor board meetings.

I accepted, and as I hung up, I said to myself, "He's going to tell me they've bought Zeiss, and they're catching up on us."

When I got to the restaurant, I was prepared for an eventful evening. I was with Patrick Cherrier, head of Essilor's Asian operations. For 15 years, both of us had worked tirelessly to expand our activities in Asia. Basically, it had been a long hard battle against Hoya, an extremely creative, powerful and determined rival. The group's president, Sato-san, is one of the most brilliant, visionary and efficient businessmen I have ever met. He is sometimes uncompromising, but always extremely fair. I remember in particular his conduct during the Iraq war. As a French company, we had a difficult time in the United States. Hoya forbade their sales teams to use our position for strategic purposes. Not a single word did the company utter against us.

We had very rarely met each other. The last time we had seen each other was in 2000, when I paid a courtesy visit to Hoya to tell them about our joint venture with Nikon. I did not want Sato-san to learn about it in the press. I wanted to give him time to break the news to his team.

Obviously, the Nikon Essilor joint venture was a blow to Sato-san. He hit back one year later by buying the biggest group of independent laboratories in the US, an acquisition we had been eyeing ourselves. It was his way of getting even. I am convinced that he waited until we were on a level playing field before giving me his news.

When we arrived at the restaurant, he said to me, "I want to tell you something I haven't said to anyone. I'm retiring. Only President Suzuki (Hoya's Chairman and CEO) knows. I wanted you to be the second person to find out." He thanked me for telling him about Nikon Essilor and said, "I'm going to admit something to you. We were both made managers at our companies at about the same time. For the last 15 years, I've woken up thinking 'I'm going to destroy Essilor, I'm going to destroy Fontanet.' Well, with hindsight, I wanted to tell you that, after 15 years, even though we didn't see each other often, I know you very well, and I feel closer to you than to many of my acquaintances, even Japanese ones."

You can imagine how I felt: I had tears in my eyes. So did Patrick Cherrier.

I let one minute pass and replied, "I also want to tell you something I haven't told anyone, Mr. Sato. Without you, without the pressure you put on us, Essilor would not be what it is today. I really think that, and I want you to know it."

There is nothing better than competition to encourage growth, strength, progress, good management and innovation. I have always been fascinated by the big rivalries in tennis, my favorite sport. Björn Borg would never have been great without John McEnroe, Chris Evert would never have succeeded without Martina Navratilova, and Roger Federer would never have triumphed without Rafael Nadal. Opposition builds champions. With no rivals, there are no champions. Rallies do not help players progress, big finals do. Without rivals, you no longer exist.

The intense and unrelenting competition in the optical sector benefited all those who wear glasses. The result was global progress in the ophthalmic optics field. Competition motivates companies and benefits consumers.

This competition between companies benefits from technological competition between countries, which is founded on local market trends and industrial strengths.

The Japanese have bigger eyes, and are more affected by near-sightedness than Europeans. Lenses correcting myopia have thick edges and lack elegance. Consequently, the Japanese have focused on producing thinner lenses by having their chemical industry develop monomers – essential elements in lens production – with very high indices. As European and US chemists were unable to imitate this technology, the Japanese had a competitive advantage. Europeans have smaller eyes than the Japanese. For this reason, more people are affected by far-sightedness. Lenses that treat far-sightedness are very complex from an optical point of view and require good math skills. To design these lenses, you need a combination of logic (to solve equations) and intuition (to make the right compromises). It is not a simple exercise. In addition, European machinery is extremely sophisticated.

Europeans are better at math than the Japanese. Maybe the Greek philosophers taught us the art of abstraction. In any case, Bernard Maitenaz invented progressive lenses, which allow better visual acuity at all distances and are a major advantage for us.

Competition meant we used their thin lenses, and they used our mathematical calculations. The opposition of Essilor and Hoya was just the tip of the iceberg: it hid a competition between two nations, two continents even. The meeting of these two continents – and the friction between two leaders – created value. Globalization can lead to progress, when the market brings these rivals together.

There is a message behind competition. Nadal's game is not the same as Federer's. The beauty in their matches is precisely because of this difference. Both players have progressed by adapting to new surfaces. Because they are able to play anywhere, their game has reached a level where it benefits everyone. Thanks to them, tennis has become so thrilling it has gained new supporters.

This is exactly what happens with business on the global level. Competitors arrive on the scene, shaped by their own histories and local markets. Their interaction with other rivals makes the industry progress and, by extension, other industries, as consumers have to make trade-offs when spending their money.

The thinness, transparency and lightness of our lenses are such that customers forget they are wearing them. This has helped our ophthalmic lenses successfully compete against contact lenses in some markets.

Globalization is an extraordinary opportunity for progress for those who take the plunge. It is also what makes the private sector strong: its field of action is global, while the public sector is only active on a national level. You can imagine what a difference this makes in management terms. Companies help us adapt to globalization, while governments claim to protect us from it.

This juxtaposition is also true of industries. We offer visual acuity, and we will be able to considerably improve on our offer with technological progress. This in turn helps the telecommunications industry, by allowing more people to read text on small screens. This supports our implantation in developing countries. Those who travel a lot know that beside every mobile phone store is an optician.

I've only mentioned the visible part of our lenses, but competition has brought us head to head in many other domains: production, IT systems, and business models. All areas of company activity have been affected.

At Essilor, everyone is responsible for company excellence. When you are one of the top companies, all staff members must perform well. Everyone at Essilor knows and accepts this. Competition makes everyone progress; not just managers. It is good stress that we deal with and that drives us… because we trust each other.

Like champions, competitors must live ascetically. Competition requires a healthy lifestyle that some see as overly restrictive. However, it is also what creates growth and gives work its epic dimension. It uncovers the talents that an average working life would leave unused.

Competition can lead to a kind of joy or pleasure when luck, a cool head and self-awareness combine to allow individuals to take on and use the stress associated with big opportunities to their advantage. Great champions need great opportunities to give their all. And, competition keeps you young – take it from someone who knows!

IS WHAT YOU DO MORAL?

"What you do is good, Mr. Fontanet, but is it moral?"

This statement was addressed to me one fall evening about 10 years ago, when I was speaking at a conference.

Generally, the first few minutes at a conference set the tone. They give you time to take the audience's pulse. That evening, I knew straight away the audience was with me. But at the end of the conference, I got a question from someone who was visibly annoyed. He attacked our profit forecast, saying something along the lines of, "financial analysts are crazy, they'll destroy everything." Essilor is committed to making a profit, because it guarantees independence – I admit it freely. I also enjoy reasoned debate and contradiction.

"I couldn't agree more, but can you tell me what you do for a living?" I replied.

"I'm retired."

"Would you be willing to go and see your pension fund and ask them to reduce your monthly payments by half so the companies it has invested in (which fund your payments) can make less profit?"

One point for me. The man did not know what to say, and the audience was smiling.

Another man got up and criticized the internationalization of production, and Essilor's policy in this field.

"Sir, can I take a look at your watch?" It was made in China.

"May I see where your suit was made?" Indonesia.

Everyone started to laugh, and I felt a little elated at my victory. I felt like I had got my message across.

Then a third man stood up – a wise man, with authority. "Mr. Fontanet, it's enthralling. I've never seen someone defend the market economy with such intelligence. But what you do, is it moral?"

Boom. My mind went blank. I eventually said I was not a philosopher, I was just in operations, and that those kinds of issues were beyond me. I felt the audience switch sides.

Because I was unable to answer this fundamental question, all my previous arguments were worthless. If you are unable to say that what you do is moral, by default, what you do is immoral. It is infallible logic.

I was thrown. There were a few more questions, then the conference ended on a sober note. It was late. I went home shaken by the episode. But at least the question pushed me to reflect on what I do on a daily basis. That is the interest in this type of experience.

The answer I should have given: "Your question is illogical."

Of course, since then, I have thought about the question. I got out my philosophy books. It was André Comte-Sponville who gave me an answer, with his book *Le Capitalisme est-il moral?* (*Is Capitalism Moral?*).

Comte-Sponville distinguishes between four different orders: the technical and economic order, the legal and political order, the ethical and moral order, and the religious order for believers.

It is important to not confuse the different orders, and apply criteria relevant to each.

In the technical and economical order, things are judged on facts. "Capitalism creates wealth, but it also creates inequalities." The legal order evaluates actions: "Something is either legal or illegal." Morality is a personal affair: moral rules are stricter than the law because we think things are better like that. Mixing the technical and economical, legal and moral orders makes no sense. I should therefore have replied to man's question with, "Your question is illogical because you are mixing up two different orders."

The market economy is neither moral nor immoral – it is amoral. It is up to each of us to do our best to act morally within this framework.

When people ask me what they should do in delicate situations, I answer that my actions have always been guided by two simple principles: one from the Bible, and the other from Emmanuel Kant. The first is, "Do unto others as you would have them do unto you," and the second is, "Act only according to that maxim whereby you can, at the same time, will that it should become a universal law.[1]"

The first principal is widely known. It exists in some form in most civilizations.

The second deserves more analysis. It reminds me of the story of the Ring of Gyges, as told by Plato. It asks whether you would act the same way if you were invisible. Would you seduce the queen and slay the king if you had a ring that made you invisible?

Today, it is the media that makes you visible. The media also presents people's words and deeds to their audiences, so the latter can judge whether a maxim should become a universal law.

In other words, if you want to know whether you are acting morally, you should ask yourself: "Would I do this if it was published in tomorrow's newspaper?"

In my opinion, Kant's principle is also valid for the media. "I just published an article. Would I do the same if the public knew how I got my information and how I decided to write the article?"

Journalists have a huge responsibility to be transparent. This should make them think about the trade-offs they make on a daily basis between speed, scoops and precision – between profitability and the expensive quest for truth.

They should know that they play an essential role in building a trusting and trustworthy society.

Playing with words destroys meaning

If economic liberalism has lost one thing, it is the battle of words. This wordplay has confused our thinking.

In France, left-wing politicians have chosen the moral high road. Consequently, the right wing has come to incarnate management,

---

1. Kant, Immanuel; translated by James W. Ellington [1785] (1993). Grounding for the Metaphysics of Morals 3rd ed.. Hackett. p. 30. ISBN 0-87220-166-X.

efficiency and greed, and the left generosity, kindness and morality. Seen from this perspective, who would want to vote right?

This hides some spurious intellectual reasoning, which deserves our attention.

French left-wing parties gained their monopoly over the heart by being the first to talk about generosity. This was one of François Mitterrand's brilliant political exploits. But is it really generous to redistribute other people's money, and not your own? I know left-leaning politicians who argue that increasing taxes for the rich is a moral and generous act. Despite this intellectual dishonesty, for the French, the heart is on the left. Because of this, being right-wing equals being selfish – and it is difficult to argue with such a well-established idea.

Left-wing politicians have also misappropriated the word "justice." For someone like me, justice means upholding the law. But, in yet another semantic shift, the left wing has carried off another political *tour de force*. Since the early 1970s, justice has also come to mean distribution. Justice is the best way of redistributing income – in other words, taking from some to give more to others. This completely negates property rights. Where are we? What have words become? Justice, a word that used to mean the upholding of property law, is now used to deny property rights.

There is even now such a thing as "fiscal justice" (a new combination), which consecrates redistribution and can be used to make some pillage "moral."

I also dislike the term "social justice". I am completely in favor of social harmony, but I do not like describing it in such a way as to imply it depends on the law and state intervention.

Recently I heard a senior level civil servant from Paris town hall say, "Bus lanes mean justice!" He meant that bus lanes create a balance between private and public modes of transport. The confusion between justice and equality is obvious.

The word "justice" has lost all meaning. So has "freedom." Since France introduced a law creating the 35-hour work week, freedom has come to mean free time. And yet another example is "solidarity." The "solidarity of striking rail workers" is really just corporatism.

Justice, solidarity and freedom: three words that have taken on new meanings.

Right-wing politicians have lost the battle of words in France, which means the country is running a big risk. The battle dates back to the demonstrations of 1968. In fact, France has lost a lot of ground with this affair. When words lose their meaning, they create endless quarrels.

For this reason, I am one of those entrepreneurs that call for more economics at high school, but also more philosophy – as long as our children learn about more than just Marxism. It is impossible to take sides in this battle of words without going back to the foundations of economic liberalism.

Why not go even further and call for more classes overall, and better French classes! I am all for Literature classes. We urgently need to work on our vocabulary.

Socrates is an excellent role model. Whenever he took part in public debates in Athens, he began by defining the words he used. What are we talking about? What do we mean by that? This was his approach whether using complex and abstract words (like justice) or simple and concrete words (like table or cave). This simple step helps avoid confusion, which can lead conversations to degenerate. Pascal said, "I do not discuss words before defining them." This applies to all civilizations throughout the ages. After being asked by the Chinese emperor what the best way was to stop civil unrest, Confucius replied, "Men need dictionaries."

Do not be fooled: those who create discord and confusion, the demagogues and the smooth talkers, twist words for their own benefit. They live off the ruins of this language, as they prosper in a society without clear and stable points of reference. To destroy a country or a civilization, there is nothing more effective than destroying its language.

In France, people have sought to associate the term "economic liberalism" with the sins of the earth, and tried to convince others that socialism is moral by mixing up different orders. This twisting of words and their meanings makes discussion impossible – in the same way that lies destroy trust.

PART III

A SHORT GUIDE TO ECONOMICS

A SHORT GUIDE TO ECONOMICS I:
UNDERSTANDING COMPETITION

The next three chapters will focus on economics, and may be tough going for some of you. We will work through them together. You can skip them if you prefer, but their aim is to help you adopt a new way of thinking about economics. These economic theories were developed some 50 years ago, and practiced before they were preached. It is based on surprisingly simple concepts that work – as I can confirm. This integrated approach combines economics and finance – the right kind of finance – and is the basis of strategies used by some of the biggest international groups. It should be taught in high school so students are better prepared for the competitive world they will have to live in.

Indeed, by accepting to live in a free society, you also accept competition. The French economist Frédéric Bastiat even said that competition was another word for freedom. This competition can sometimes be frightening, but it can also encourage personal development. Whether you like it or not, competition is a fact – it affects everyone. Those who understand it best will be those who succeed in the future.

Thanks to the economist Bruce Henderson, major progress has been made in this field. Henderson founded the Boston Consulting Group (BCG) in 1963, and was probably the first competition theorist.

In particular, he was the first to understand cost and price dynamics in competitive markets. He discovered the relationship between sales and investment. He also looked into the link between profit and growth, and identified simple numerical constants that apply to all economic sectors.

Armed with these tools, Henderson developed a logical and practical way of applying this strategy, which the BCG called optimizing resource allocation (human and financial resources) in competitive markets.

Mostly, he sold this strategy to companies that came to him for advice. Because some of the world's biggest companies have been applying this strategy for over 40 years, these ideas have been instrumental in creating leaders on the global market. However, they are not well known to the public or academics, and they are only taught in a few business schools. This is a real shame, because his ideas are easy to understand and could help prepare students for the world they will have to live in.

I was fortunate enough to join BCG when these ideas were in the development stage. I have used them for over 30 years in our operations. They have helped me a lot, and I can confidently say they work.

For these reasons, I would like to present the basics of this theory here, and demonstrate some of its practical uses.

The first element is what we call the "experience curve".

The experience curve

Everyone understands that as companies increase production, their costs decrease.

The best way of measuring this decrease is not by taking the company's yearly production, as economists have done until now, but by taking cumulative production since the company began. Henderson called this cumulative production "experience."

The curve's slope appears to be fixed over time: the costs of value-added (costs less purchases) measured at constant prices drop 20 to 25% each time accumulated experience doubles, whatever the industry.

So, if a company grows at a rate of 15% (extremely quickly), its experience doubles in five years. Its costs of value-added drop 25%, or 5% every year, over the same period.

If, however, a company grows at a rate of 3% (the normal speed), its experience will not double for 25 years, and its costs will drop only

1% every year. In other words, five times slower than in the previous example.

The curve's slope is the same for both companies: what changes is the rate at which they accumulate experience and therefore reduce costs.

Another key finding was that in the same industry all the firms were on the same curve at the same time (if, of course, factor costs are excluded).[1] Basically, an industry's experience curve is like a staircase: everyone has to go down it, but not everyone is on the same step.

Henderson's theories have been confirmed in studies carried out around the world over the last 40 years. In each case, these studies show that competitors in an industry have different costs despite producing similar products.

This had a surprising consequence: competitors do not have the same profit margins on the same product, and these differences can be quite significant. For example, imagine an industry where three competitors have market shares of 40%, 20% and 10% respectively. After a certain period of time, their experience becomes proportional to their market share. As a result, the market leader's value-added costs will be 25% lower than the second competitor, whose value-added costs will be 25% lower than the third.

You might think that competitors in the same business have the same costs. Not at all! For example, a sale may be much more profitable for one car manufacturer than another, even though the vehicle works just as well in both cases.

At the time, these ideas represented real conceptual progress in microeconomics. However, the academic world paid them little attention. This is probably why Henderson was never nominated for the Nobel Prize in economics, even though he deserved it in my opinion.

Segmentation (defining businesses) and life cycles

Experience curves apply to a "business." A business is a competitive system where goods or services are produced for consumers.

---

1. See Appendices, T 2.

The business requires technical expertise that companies improve on as they acquire experience. The definition of "business" is relatively precise: it is neither a sector nor an industry (manufacturing products and processes, transportation and forestry, for example). The difference is subtler. Everyone understands that aircraft, vehicle and train manufacturing are different businesses. The companies and expertise required differ enormously. Today, the global automotive business includes both small and large cars, because competitors produce a full range of vehicles. However, there is a difference between car and truck businesses. Companies choose to specialize in one or the other. If they decide to produce both, they set up completely separate divisions.

Today there are around 50 million companies in the world, which means there are a huge number of businesses. There are rarely more than ten competitors per business, which means there are millions of businesses worldwide. In this Henderson agrees with Hayek, who was the first to underline the varied nature of the economy by using the concept *catallaxy* (meaning both variety and change in Greek).

Businesses have a geographical aspect: they are local, national, continental or global. Businesses usually start out by being local and, as companies expand geographically, become continental and then global. Product businesses generally expand faster than service businesses.

Businesses also have a life cycle: growth starts out slowly before speeding up, stabilizing, slowing down and eventually contracting. A business life cycle can be anywhere from ten years to hundreds of years. The steel and flat glass businesses, for example, have been around for 300 years, while thermoplastics have only been around 50. Some businesses just simply disappear (as was the case for stagecoaches, clippers and steam locomotives).

The business life cycle was discovered by Schumpeter. An expanding business replaces a contracting business or businesses. Overall, businesses are increasingly numerous as the market economy spreads around the world.

The battle between businesses can be head-on, with one replacing the other – when the car replaced the stagecoach or the electric light bulb replaced the candle, for instance. Many businesses can compete for the same customers – as do rail travel, air travel and automobiles in trips of over 500 miles. The number of competing businesses can be high – consider, for example, the different businesses competing with Apple's iPhone.

Technology plays an important role in business life cycles. Encyclopedias were first printed on paper (for example, the Encyclopedias Diderot, Britannica and Quid), then recorded on CD-ROMs (for example, Encarta), before being accessed on the Internet (for example, Wikipedia, which is written by users themselves). Businesses can adapt to technological change or be destroyed by it. Traditional encyclopedias were leaders when it came to digitalization, but were unable to keep up during the Internet age. Technological change is restructuring businesses in all sectors of the economy.

Modern economies are therefore hives of activity that cannot be compared to chaos. We will discuss this more in the next chapter. This activity is governed by rules that appear to be a kind of natural order. Once again, this is counterintuitive, because an "order" suggests the presence of policemen or regulators. Nevertheless, this natural order has its rules, and very clear trends emerge for those equipped with the right tools, as we will see.

Market share and price dynamics

Once companies understand the life cycle and cost difference principles, their strategy is simple. They try to increase their market share as quickly as possible, in order to advance along the experience curve where their costs are lower than those of their competitors.

The only problem for these companies is that most competitors have the same goal. The battle for the top spots is tough, and this is what leads to lower costs for the consumer.

The smartest companies, those which best understand how the curve works, lead at the end of the business life cycle. The battle can last decades. The winners are those that are global players and know how to put their past experience to (best) use.

Because market prices tend to stay the same for all competitors while costs differ, profit margins can vary considerably. The market leader is more profitable than the runner up, and the runner up is more profitable than the company in third position. These differences can last a long time. It is therefore essential to understand how competitors with different profit margins can coexist in the long term.[2]

Return on capital and asset turnover

Henderson's second major breakthrough was in finance. It relies on a precise definition of the terms return and investment.

Companies must invest to survive. Most people without experience in business believe that successful companies are built around a good product. This is a good idea, but wrong nonetheless. No matter how good a product is, it does not ensure a company's success. Companies must also finance the plant that produces the product. For the product to be successful, then, there must be some form of investment.

This investment can be in plants or in working capital (inventory and accounts receivable minus accounts payable), but it requires money. When companies expand because their products sell well, they must increase investment. While yearly activity is measured in turnover, investment can be measured at any time as the value of plants in operation and the working capital required to get products to customers.

Henderson discovered that there is a relationship between sales revenue and investment (named asset turnover) in each industry. This has been confirmed in thousands of business studies carried out worldwide.

In addition, the studies showed that this relationship remains stable over time. In other words, investment grows at the same rate as sales revenue. This may seem obvious, but Henderson was the first to identify it.

This discovery has important implications because it allows us to establish a simple relationship between profits and growth. First, however, let us define return on capital.

Imagine a company that has no debts and profits amounting to 15% of sales after taxes. This is its profit margin, or profitability.

Now, suppose that in this industry $1 invested amounts to $1 in sales revenue (as is the case in the chemicals industry, for example). In

---

2. See Appendices, T 3.

this situation, the margin calculated with respect to investment – rather than sales – is also 15%. This is return on capital.

Consider another industry – the sailing industry, which we will examine in more detail later on. In this industry, asset turnover is 2. Each $1 invested amounts to $2 in sales revenue. If profits after taxes are 15% of sales, the company's return on capital is 30%. A return of 15% is obtained with a 7.5% margin on sales revenue after taxes.

It is much more relevant to talk about return on capital than profitability, because entrepreneurs make decisions based on the capital they contribute to the company to finance investment. What matters to them is return on capital, not profit margins (or profitability).

This way of thinking has another advantage: it allows us to establish a link between profits and growth.

Return on capital, dividends and growth

Henderson's third breakthrough was establishing a simple relationship between return on capital, dividends and growth.

Let us come back to our company with a 15% return on capital. If no dividends are paid out to the business owner, this sum is reinvested in the company. This allows the owner to increase investment and sales revenue by 15% (because asset rotation remains constant). Thus, if no dividends are paid out, companies grow at the same rate as their return on capital.

If 50% of profits are paid out in dividends, the owner can only reinvest 7.5% (50% of 15%). The company's growth will be 7.5%.

If 100% of the profits are paid out in dividends, the company will not grow.[3]

In other words, return on capital gives an idea of the maximum growth a company can attain. Actual growth depends on how much is paid out in dividends. Dividends therefore form part of a company's strategy, as they determine how fast it advances along the experience curve.

In this situation, market leaders have an advantage, because they have the most experience and are located at the bottom of the curve.

---

3. See Appendices, T 4.

They therefore have the fastest growth potential. If leaders are aware of their market share and its value, they are very difficult to dislodge. Relative market share is the real measure of a company's value.

This relationship between dividends and growth also explains the following paradox: "how do competitors with different rates of return coexist in the same industry?" The answer is simple: dividend payouts play the regulatory role. Leaders are able to pay out dividends and keep growing, but followers cannot if they wish to maintain their market share. The leaders' sshareholders recover more than their investment, and the others lose it.

In other words, the cash flows (profits minus reinvestment) of companies in the same business are completely different. Some competitors can pay regular dividends, while others cannot. This state of affairs can last decades.[4]

From dividends to cash flows

Cash flows incorporate dividends, but also money paid by shareholders into the company.

As we have seen, return on capital measures a company's maximum possible growth, which is regulated by dividends. Dividends can be seen as flows exiting companies. If a company does not grow, it can pay out 15% in cash instead of investing. If it grows 7.5%, it can pay out 7.5% in cash instead of investing. If it grows 15%, it does not pay out anything.

Consequently, if shareholders receive no dividends but instead pay 10% of assets into the company, the company grows 25%.

Managing these flows makes it possible to control the rate at which the company grows.

Consider, for example, a normal company that has a return on capital of 5%.

This rate of return is much more common than the 15% above, generally reserved for companies at the bottom of the experience curve. In this example, the company is unable to increase returns above 5%.

---

4. See Appendices, T 5.

What happens if the market growth rate is 10%? The company has two options. Either it pays a small dividend of 2%, for example, meaning growth is limited to 3% (5% less 2%). As a result, it loses market share, because the industry is growing faster than the company. It will not advance along the experience curve fast enough and, inevitably, its return on capital will drop. The company will go out of business or be sold.

Or the company can aim for growth of 15%, 5% faster than the market rate. This means finding an investor willing to inject 10% every year to make up the shortfall in investment. This 10% external investment added to the 5% investment generated internally allows the company to grow 15%. It is on its way to becoming a leader.

Catching up in an industry is therefore possible, but it requires cash from outside the company.

Cash flows within and between businesses

Cash flows determine behavior in competitive systems. Strategy is nothing more than the art of managing these flows during the business life cycle. Generally speaking, a good strategy consists in reinvesting profits until the company has become a market leader and the business is experiencing stable growth. At this point, paying out big dividends is no longer a problem. Payouts are even wise because they avoid the waste of precious resources. Just make sure followers are not using the opportunity to catch up to you (see the Beneteau example).

Companies can diversify by diverting flows from one business to another. In this situation, the company is said to have a portfolio of activities. Shareholders can also divert flows between businesses by using their dividends to invest in promising new companies.

It is clear that this flow from stable companies to the rest of the economy is essential. It is this money that finances start-ups. It is a way of investing in the future of the economy.

The next step is the exciting subject of portfolio management, developed by Henderson but which is beyond the scope of this book. There is a lot of information available on this topic, and an essential reading list features at the end of this book.

Conclusion

Bruce Henderson managed to create a simple and coherent conceptual system. Thanks to him, corporate strategy has made a lot of progress. He also developed a conceptual framework, which has inspired large companies for the last 40 years. Judge for yourselves whether it should be included in school curriculums!

His work has been extremely useful for companies. Good strategies are key to building trust: they help companies analyze the market situation, reduce uncertainty and build strong teams.

These teams are perfectly capable of understanding corporate strategy and making contributions to it. It goes without saying that good strategies must be understood by all before they can be well implemented.

Just as a good strategy is not sufficient to ensure success, a bad strategy will not work even if well implemented. In today's world, a two-pronged approach is necessary: trust is required to implement strategies, and strategies build trust.

Thanks, Bruce!

A SHORT GUIDE TO ECONOMICS II: THE LITTLE PIGS THEORY

I met Philippe Durand-Daguin and Jacques Roux at Wagons-Lits when I took charge of its catering branch Eurest and food services to public institutions in 1986.

Jacques and Philippe were in charge of branch operations. They had launched these businesses. I enjoyed my time working with them, even if our complicated shareholding arrangements meant we were unable to fully realize our potential. They taught me the ins and outs of the service industry. I am very grateful to them.

Catering is a service business, and entirely focused on customers. Catering companies are awarded service contracts to run operations for customer companies. The caterers hire kitchen staff, buy raw materials and charge employers and employees for meals eaten in cafeterias. These contracts run from three months to three years, rarely longer. When they expire, catering companies re-submit bids for the contracts.

Contract catering companies can be very large, because they employ a large number of staff and require very little investment. As a result, they grow quickly. The only limits are competition and how quickly customers subcontract. Clients include companies, schools and hospitals. By 1985, the companies we ran served several million meals per day and employed tens of thousands of people.

BCG's theories have been criticized for not applying to services. Critics argue that it is impossible to build an experience curve without products. However, in service businesses, it quickly becomes clear that some contracts have better margins than others. It is also obvious that some competitors do much better than others in terms of profit and growth. This is living proof that competitive advantages are also a reality in service businesses.

The experience curve is a learning tool demonstrating competitive advantages for different products. The little pigs theory shows how companies develop competitive advantages in the service industry.

Little pigs

When I was with BCG in the late 1970s, I worked for René Monory at the Ministry of Finance. My role was to look into compensation payments to pig farmers that exported their products.

These payments compensated the fact that, by law, they had to use raw materials from the European Union, which cost more than other raw materials on the world market. The Minister of Finance was concerned that compensation payments were increasing because pig farmers exported more. There were also big industrial piggery projects, which cost a lot of money and were unprofitable. René Monory asked us to report on the industry's competitiveness. I therefore looked into the pig farming industry throughout Europe.

I quickly realized that the industry was only growing in three regions in Europe: Denmark, Holland and France (Brittany, to be precise).

An initial analysis showed that the pig production growth rates in these regions was directly linked to the density of pigs per square kilometer. The explanation for this was very simple, as is always the case for really important issues.

Pig farmers, being specialists, reinvested their profits by building new piggeries. You could almost estimate farmers' profits based on their growth. As pork is a commodity and sold at the same price throughout Europe, high growth means high investment and high profits, therefore low costs. As growth was strongest in areas with high pig densities, it meant that costs dropped proportionally as density increased. In other words, the higher the density, the lower the costs.

In this example, then, product "experience" as identified by Bruce Henderson was geographical density in the region the company operated in.

Geographical density meant it cost less to produce more pigs because the region was already home to bigger feed factories and slaughterhouses, and its pig farmers had better technical expertise from learning from each other. This is the "density" effect.

Finally, in countries like France, prices doubled between dense and less dense regions. Big industrial piggeries had been set up in regions with low density, and their large-scale production could not make up for the effects of density. Even though a considerable amount of money had been injected into these operations, they were not competitive.

Cafeterias and the little pigs theory

The same principles applied to cafeterias. In regions with more cafeterias, companies had a denser logistical network that allowed them to reduce costs compared to their competitors.

Technical expertise was also better, because technicians could visit several sites in the same day. This had an immediate effect on production costs. We could sell at lower prices, earn more profit at market prices, or serve better quality food. We chose the latter option.

Density was also a commercial advantage. Our reputation spread faster by word of mouth in denser regions. Eurest had a very good reputation and our clients were our best salespeople. As soon as our cafeteria density reached a certain threshold, it became much easier to win contracts, whether for staff, school or hospital cafeterias.

Our competitors all sought to specialize in a different product (school cafeterias, instead of hospitals, for example), while we sought to be the regional leader. It was an effective strategy!

To explain the value of density, which is not intuitive and requires some explaining, we came up with the "little pigs strategy." It was amusing, and everyone understood what we meant.

Our strategy was therefore to have a higher cafeteria density than our competitors. Traditionally, Eurest was strong in the Paris region, as the company was launched at La Défense. It was our most profitable region. We now needed to prove that the strategy, which was purely theoretical, could work in practice.

To show our teams the value of geographic density, we decided to launch an offensive on the cafeterias on the Ile de la Cité, in Paris' historical center. It was proof of our good intentions, but also an excellent way of communicating with our customers and employees.

We waged major battles with our competitors. We began by taking key locations in central Paris such as the Hôtel-Dieu, the Palais de Justice and the Préfecture de Police. Our sweetest victory was no doubt the contract to cater for the clergy at the Archevêché. What better blessing for our strategy?

A SHORT GUIDE TO ECONOMICS III: UNDERSTANDING THE FUTURE

Catallactics and creative destruction are two concepts that will help Europeans analyze future events.

Most importantly, they help us understand that the market is an extremely sophisticated mechanism that is controlled by a natural order. There have been distortions, but that does not mean we should throw out the baby with the bathwater.

Catallaxy is a very clear way of describing the economy that explains why some people succeed while others struggle. This difference is often due to the economic sector they work in.

In Europe, changes in habits and tastes have coincided with a period of intense technological change. Consequently, the economy will have to be completely overhauled. It is unlikely that developed countries will experience strong growth in the next 15 years. However, there will be considerable differences in growth rates between new and aging economic sectors. This transformation, which respects the notion of "creative destruction," will require considerable flexibility from European populations. Many will change companies. Investment will have to focus on new industries.

The national economy is not just about GDP and growth. It incorporates what are probably hundreds of thousands of niche markets that are expanding, stagnating or contracting. In this context, niche markets and businesses – defined in the previous chapter – are two words for the same thing. Despite the fact that growth in Western countries will probably be weak, there will be considerable changes in the economy as people move between expanding and contracting businesses.

Three authors, whose work is relatively unknown to the general public, can help us understand the relationship between GDP and companies.

They are Hayek, who described catallaxy (modern economies are not monolithic but made up of hundreds of thousands of different businesses or niche markets); Schumpeter, who spread the "creative destruction" idea; and Bruce Henderson, who developed insights into the equilibrium of companies in the same business and cash flows between different businesses.

Catallactics

In economics, relatively little attention is paid to the large number of companies making up the modern economy. This has always surprised me. The number of companies is revealing.

Has anyone ever wondered why there are 2.5 million companies in France alone? This figure includes all companies, including sole proprietors. Over 500,000 companies have over ten employees. This is a huge number!

Modern economies provide an immense range of goods and services. This seems so normal to us we rarely pay them attention. Before you get to work in the morning, you have already used goods and services produced by thousands of companies. You wash yourself (health and beauty industry), take medication (pharmaceutical industry), eat breakfast (processed foodstuffs industry), listen to the radio or read the newspaper (media), drive or take public transportation to work (transportation industry) and look at what time it is (watch-making industry). All of your activities are watched over by insurance companies. You may have withdrawn cash at an ATM machine, or done any one of a number of other activities. Those listed thus far are mostly in the private sector. The public sector ensures our safety, provides public transportation and so on. In other words, modern economies are much more complex mechanisms than we think they are. We do not appreciate what we have.

Consider how much imagination and energy it takes to supply a city like Paris with fresh food. Just think what is needed in terms of information systems, logistics, storage and labeling. These activities are complex and very well run. Food shortages are rare (we would hear about them in the news if there were any). Given consumer demand, this is proof that our complex distribution system works.

How many different niche markets are there? If there are approximately five competitors per niche, there are around 100,000 (500,000 divided by 5) different niche markets in economies like the French one.

Each niche market has its own momentum. They are expanding, stable or contracting. A modern economy is like a field of wildflowers, with an incredible variety of grasses, plants, insects, dirt, organic matter, minerals, earthworms and bacteria. The grass and flowers are most visible, but they need many less visible suppliers (like dirt and insects). All these elements are necessary. Without them, the field would disappear.

Consumers have the real power, because they make choices. These decisions take place daily when it comes to consumer goods, or are spaced out over several years for durable goods. Consumers have the power over product life cycles. They make life or death (expansion or contraction) decisions.

This is something we are not always aware of when we are at supermarket checkouts. Nevertheless, our day-to-day choices determine companies' fates.

Planned economies were unable to deal with this boom in niche markets. This was one of the reasons the Berlin Wall fell. It is difficult to implement an industrial strategy in economies with so many sectors. There are too many niches to choose from!

The question that is generally asked is "how do we manage this extraordinary complexity?"

But are things really so chaotic? Should the economy be left to regulate itself or should the government step in? How do we explain what happens between companies in a niche market and what happens between the niches themselves?

To answer these questions, we must examine two concepts: equilibrium and movement.

Equilibrium in niche markets

When a niche market is at the beginning of the life cycle, there are many different competitors and no company dominates. Leaders never stay ahead for long because market share is won and lost easily when markets grow quickly. This situation lasts as long as market growth is strong (above 10%). When growth starts to slow, a stable hierarchy usually emerges. This includes a leader, a few followers, and smaller competitors.

Leaders are generally twice as large as their closest followers, and have a much better return on capital (15% as opposed to 5%). The companies in positions 3, 4 and 5 are often half the size of the biggest follower and make very little money – they rarely stay independent for long.

In practice, market share distribution varies depending on the niche, and is only visible after a certain period of time. It is a bit like a cycling race: at the beginning, all the riders are in the peloton but, by the end of the stage, the best riders are out in front.

It is like an aquarium that fish have been living in for a while. There is generally one big fish, several medium-sized fish and a whole school of small fish.

Schumpeter and movement

After some time has passed, the competitors in niche markets reach equilibrium. This means growth has fallen and the niche market is at risk of being replaced by another niche market. As growth is weak, productivity increases stabilize and prices can drop no further because costs will drop no further. This is the perfect opportunity for new businesses. Equilibrium in the existing niche is relatively stable, while the niche situation becomes precarious. Past examples of this phenomenon include candles and light bulbs, stagecoaches and cars, typewriters and word processing programs, steel and chemistry, hunting/fishing and farming, landlines and mobile phones.

Competition between unrelated niche markets can also occur when consumers make trade-offs while spending their budget. For example, the rise in mobile phone contracts appears to have brought about a drop in cheese purchases in France. Salaries only go so far, so consumers cannot continually increase spending.

These new products and trade-offs result from changes in taste and new technologies. Their effects are difficult to predict, but are always determined by consumers. This is what Schumpeter calls "creative destruction" – because there is always something new to replace the old.

Schumpeter left unresolved the question of how these niche markets were financed. This is where the BCG's net cash flows come in.

Bruce Henderson and cash flows

To understand the cash flow mechanism, you need to know what a company's assets are (see A Short Guide to Economics I).

Demand for investment can be measured using a simple equation: assets multiplied by growth. In light industry, for example, $100 million in sales revenue requires $50 million in assets (industrial capital plus stock plus working capital). If the industry grows by 10% every year, sales revenue will grow by $10 million, and assets will need to be increased by $5 million to keep up. Another way of calculating this is as follows: assets are worth $50 million, the industry is growing by 10%, therefore companies must set aside 10% of $50 million each year – $5 million – to finance investment.

Start-ups need much more money than they generate. Observers outside the industry often underestimate these financing needs. New businesses grow 20 to 25% each year. Every year, they need to increase their assets by 20 to 25%. Because of competition, it is very rare for start-ups to earn sufficient return on capital to finance their own growth. The market leader might grow by 25%, for example, but only have a return on capital of 15%. This means its cash flow is –10% (15% minus 25%). Meanwhile, the followers may not make any money, and require injections equal to 25% of their assets every year. This is a hefty sum! They need cash cows to finance their activity.

Where does this money come from in a market economy? It does not fall out of the sky or come from the government. It comes from the sectors that are being replaced – mature sectors, in other words. These sectors experience slow growth, and require very little reinvestment. Cash can be taken away from companies in these businesses without jeopardizing their market share.

Consider, for example, a mature market that grows at 2% per year. Its age means competitors are few: it resembles the fish tank we discussed earlier. There is one leader, who is twice the size of the nearest follower. This follower is twice as large as the three other companies competing for market share. The leader's return on capital is 15%, the follower's is 5% and the other companies' is 2%. As far as cash flows are concerned, the leader pays out 13% of its asset value in dividends (15% minus 2%), the follower pays out 3% (5% minus 2%), and the other companies pay out nothing. Do the math: because of its size and ability to generate cash, the leader is responsible for 90% of the industry's cash flows. This cash can be reinvested in other activities ensuring the company's growth, or paid out in dividends to shareholders, allowing them to reinvest in other areas. We always underestimate leaders' roles in financing the economy.

We must let market concentration take place. Leaders in mature businesses support sectors that are expanding by contributing cash. Dividends are therefore necessary for the economy, and should not always be frowned upon. All parts of the economy are interconnected: large stable companies support small companies that are expanding rapidly.

Leaders therefore play a key role in financing. Their financing ability is much larger than their size would indicate. They should be appreciated for their true worth.

Only leaders are able to divert cash away from mature markets for the benefit of the entire economy. Consequently, leaders with big market shares and dividends should not be feared. They should definitely not be prevented from emerging, because they are essential to a robust economy. Without leaders, the economy grows more slowly, because start-ups lack the cash they need to finance growth.

People

This movement also applies to people who change sectors. When one sector contracts, another expands (destruction is creative). Each time a job is destroyed in one area, another is created somewhere else. People are not always aware of this. Unfortunately, we are only shown the sectors that are contracting and plants that are closing. Of course, it is much simpler to show sectors that are contracting, because the companies involved are large and at the end of their life span. They are much more visible than the plethora of small companies that spring up around the country. These new companies are much harder to see. It is much more exciting to watch a forest destroyed by fire or hurricane than a field of wheat growing. It is always the same story. The exception becomes the rule.

This has a major impact on the general public. They hear which sectors are contracting, but not which sectors are expanding. People are not idiots: explaining this movement to them would significantly increase mobility.

Summing up

We should talk more about catallaxy and creative destruction.

The economy is infinitely more varied than we think it is (and this chapter has not even dealt with the variations caused by globalization). This variety does not create chaos. Competition allows people to act freely, and ensures each niche market reaches equilibrium.

Each business has a life cycle, and it is normal for companies to become fewer as the life cycle progresses. Changes in taste and technology constantly affect the equilibrium between different businesses. Dividends are subtle mechanisms that naturally enable companies to transfer cash generated by mature markets to sectors experiencing strong growth and lacking liquidity.

These market mechanisms should be explained in more detail. Too many people say, "The market is chaotic! It's utter bedlam!" Understanding market mechanisms is key to living the future in an intelligent way.

PART IV

FINANCE: GOOD OR BAD?

THE DANGER
OF SHORT TERM FINANCE

"Mr. Fontanet, I have an exciting opportunity for you. Can we meet in person?"

We have received offers like this several times. We get a call from the director of an international banking firm, who wants to meet us in person to discuss an interesting business opportunity. He generally knows Essilor well – or, more precisely, our financial statements.

In the above case, he was pleasant, to the point and dynamic on the phone. But we had a hard time figuring out what he wanted. We did not know whether to put him off, or hear him out. Thinking he might be selling one of our rivals, we decided to meet with him. It was part of our duty to monitor competition.

In situations like these both Philippe Alfroid, chief operating officer, and I attend the meetings. There is always strength in numbers. A very well known person once correctly said, "At Essilor, they hunt in packs."

The meeting began with an offer to sell a company whose business was similar to ours. Basically, the group's name had a vague reference to optics. As Essilor specializes in ophthalmic optics, we immediately realized that the company's operations were not in the same field as ours. The conversation came to a halt.

During this time, the banker had indulged in a little name-dropping to show us how wide his network was. He even mentioned a few ministers – sometimes by their first names. These tactics never work with me. It just made me wonder whether he would talk about me in the same tone after his meeting with us – as if we were close friends. I am always wary of people who are over-familiar. However, this was a professional situation, so we had to keep listening.

Then came the flattery. I hate flattery! When you like the truth, you learn to be suspicious of this very unsubtle trick. "We've had our eye on you and Philippe for a long time now. What incredible careers! We really admire you, your company is one of Europe's finest."

Then we got down to the real business.

"We'd like to get involved in your project. We could help you delist the company. You know, once you've left the stock market, there are a lot of options open to you. We have investors focused on the long term, who would let you test strategies equal to your talents." He then gave examples of successful delistings without going into too much detail – because the operations had in fact had mixed results. "The stock market is too focused on the short term. That can be very restrictive... We'd give you back your freedom... And, you know, we'd help you earn a lot of money, because you'd be shareholders."

It is not the first time someone has made us offers like this, using flattery and the enticing prospect of future wealth. Our answer has always been the same: "We're fine the way we are, we don't need to get any richer. Our priorities are our families and friends, our company, and a good working environment. Anyway, how do you plan to delist the group? Could you be a bit more precise? Can you jot down a few figures? We're not bankers, but we can understand your reasoning. We're skeptical, but convince us!"

Basically, the idea was to create a highly leveraged holding company and delist the group. As there would be very little capital, it would be easy to give directors a lot of shares. After the debt had been paid off, the investors would become very rich. The only problem was the debt itself, and paying it off.

I then spoke up. "Let's talk figures. To delist the company, we'd need to pay shareholders 30% more than the share price, or 13 billion euros ($18.3 billion). Essilor would have to run up a debt for this amount. Interest on the debt would be around 600 million euros ($846 million) per year. Our profits are around 700 million euros ($987 million). After paying off the interest, we'd have 100 million euros ($141 million) to reimburse the debt itself. If our calculations are correct, it would take us 130 years to become debt free (13 billion divided by 100 million equals 130). Our calculations are rough, but you get the idea. That's a long time."

"But you don't understand. You could sell off assets or a less strategic business."

"It's not quite as simple as that. We only make one type of product, and our mechanics divisions are essential to our strategy."

"Well, you could probably raise prices for certain products."

"If you really knew the industry, you'd know that it's extremely competitive. If we upset the market equilibrium like that we'd quickly lose market share. We have competitors who have borrowed money to take part in LBOs. They raised their prices and lost a whole lot of market share. They're currently suffering precisely because they followed this kind of strategy."

"Our group has investors who are specialists in management. If you join us, they'll help you lower your costs."

He reeled off some names.

Our immediate response was:

"You know, we're constantly going through our expenses with a fine comb. We're competing with the US, Germany, Japan, South Korea and last but certainly not least China. We spend all our time cutting costs. The consultants you just mentioned are at Essilor right now. We don't think that other consultants would necessarily do a better job. And, we're patient, but... 130 years seems like a long time to wait. Couldn't things go any faster?"

"Of course they could!"

"How?"

"By relisting the company on the stock exchange."

As simple as that!

"Anyway," we said, "it's not us you need to convince, but the 5,000 members of Valoptec. We're just the management team, we don't have any say. They decide, and if you talk to them like that, you probably won't get very far!"

That was the deciding argument. He saw that Essilor was a strange breed of company and lost heart. He probably recovered quickly – these people are made of stern stuff and quickly move on to their next audacious exploit.

We left on good terms.

"Thank you for taking an interest in us. You were right to come and see us. We don't think your idea will work at Essilor, but ours is a very strange industry. Taking on such a large debt while we are waging such a tough competitive battle seems like a very risky plan. Neither Philippe nor I would like to go down in Essilor history as the managers who destroyed the company for personal gain. Everyone knows that leverage buyouts (LBOs) involve the company contracting debt to replace shareholders. No matter what people say, the company reduces investment to pay back its debts. For well-run and profitable companies, LBOs are not only stupid, they are also potentially disastrous. If we decided to go ahead with your idea, we'd lose market share and possibly weaken the company, because our biggest rivals would jump on the opportunity to catch up to us. Sooner or later, we would be at the mercy of our competitors. We think a lot of Essilor, we like the company the way it is. Thank you very much, but it's best we leave it at that."

This kind of discussion, between the financial world and managers, has become increasingly frequent over the last decade. This does not mean I condemn all LBOs. Many have been successful, because leverage ratios were well calculated. One example is Legrand, where investors had real contributions to make when it came to improving management processes. But there have also been many risky operations. The financial crisis, because it was not forecast, finished off a lot of them.

Purely financial LBOs are a way of earning in five years what you would normally earn in 15. But, no matter what people say, they are extremely risky operations. At Essilor, we consider that you can buy space, but not time. A good friend of mine, who is at the head of another CAC 40 company with a similar outlook as ours, once said that "time always takes its toll."

"Xavier, I'm leaving XYZ. I'll tell you about it later."

G. was one of the most brilliant managers I knew in optics. For three years, he had been managing one of our competitors: XYZ. His energy was unparalleled.

He had been headhunted while working as a division manager for a large international group. He left, probably attracted by the CEO position he was offered. He thought he was going to be his own boss. He was, but only for three financial years.

Things at XYZ changed significantly when a prestigious investment fund bought shares in the company.

The fund had targeted our industry, probably thinking we had a good business. There are "good" and "bad" businesses. Good businesses are those with good profit margins, bad businesses are those without. It is as simple as that. This analysis was based on our profits. They were aiming to do as well as Essilor. G. joined XYZ as part of an LBO along the same lines as the offer put to us above. It involved created a holding company – heavily in debt – with the former shareholder and top management. He had found a backer who would fund the operation in return for half of the holding.

There was just one flaw: the debt. We knew it. This complex operation was very heavily leveraged – less than in the above example, but too heavily to be viable. The interest on the debt represented about 5 to 6% of XYZ's profit. After paying off the interest, the holding and XYZ probably only just broke even. Breaking even after financial costs was in fact the aim. This meant a minimum of ready cash was required. Investors thought the group would quickly catch up to Essilor, thanks to a management team that had proved their worth in another, much bigger industry and the fund's techniques. Once they were in position, they would sell the company and pay off the debt.

It was a nice idea but… what could G. do up against the 500 years' experience racked up by Essilor's executive committee? G. was definitely stronger, harder working, more talented, more courageous and a better businessman than each of us individually. But what chance did he have against us as a team – especially in a business as complex as ours?

As soon as the fund invested in XYZ, the company's mainstays – key staff members – retired. This was not a problem in the short term, because it lowered costs. But the company lost priceless expertise.

As time went by, XYZ's earnings did not improve. The investment fund began to get impatient. XYZ's priority was paying off its debt, so it could not invest in new technology appearing in the market. Then the financial crisis struck. The investment fund's shareholders could hold out no longer. G. paid for the mistake.

The mistake was thinking that success is just a question of good management. This is underestimating the optical industry's extraordinary complexity. To expand in this market, you must be in a position that you can only obtain through market share and experience.

Knowledge transfers between industries are difficult exercises. First and foremost, you need enough time to be able to do things properly. Five years is nothing in this business! The best timeframe is 15 to 20 years.

G. was a victim of this short-term logic. His career and reputation were unfairly affected by these events. Some of our senior staff gave in to temptation and accepted G.'s highly paid job offers. We did not want to enter into a bidding war, even though this meant losing skills and expertise. A few years later, these employees regretted their decisions and realized that experiences like these are generally of short duration.

This experience also damaged the industry, because it meant we lost a successful R&D center and a creative company, which had previously produced high quality products. Short-term finance wreaks havoc – on a much larger scale than we think it does.

To achieve great things, companies need solid long-term strategies, shareholders and CEOs. I think people are becoming aware of this, but there will have to be more havoc before they come to the right conclusions.

The long road

The road is long, so we need a solution that will go the distance: sustainable finance.

At Essilor, we have always sought to strike the right balance between financial policy (dividends and debts) and strategy (increased, steady or decreased market share). Our results have generally been good.

The ophthalmic optics market has historically grown around 3.5% every year. The sector is not expanding very rapidly, because the business has been around for a very long time. However, we have always sought to grow faster than the market – three times faster, or 10 to 11%, to be precise. Why?

Because we know the value of market share, and that companies with high market share have lower costs than their rivals. Consequently, they generate higher returns.

The value of market share can be seen in almost all industries. Gradually increasing your market share year by year, as Essilor does, creates a stable company, team and investors.

For around ten years, we have maintained our return on capital at around 17.5%. We pay out one third of our profits in dividends, and reinvest the remaining two thirds in the company (two thirds of 17.5% is around 11% – our historical growth rate for the last 20 years). We are a no-debt company and our number of shares is constant. The circle is complete.

It is like running a marathon: you have to adapt your carbohydrate intake (finance) to your pace (10 to 11% annual growth). There is no point in running faster – we do not want to create financial leverage. The aim is simply to run for as long as possible.

We could try to go faster, but what good would it do? We could play around with statistics, but we do not. It is completely out of the question for us to play around with what tens of thousands of people have taken decades to build.

Are we going to change? We do not need to. The arrival of China, India, Latin America and Africa on the market mean that our business is likely to grow for longer than we thought two years ago!

THE STOCK EXCHANGE

The Saint Gobain Story

Early in May 2000, I got a phone call from Jean-Louis Beffa, Chairman of Saint Gobain. Saint Gobain wanted to sell their stake in Essilor. He wanted things to be tied up before the end of the year. I was not particularly surprised. We had been expecting it for a while. But it still meant the end of an era.

The group had bought a stake in Essilor – at our request – back in 1987. At the time, Valoptec's control rate was falling as long-serving staff members left the company or passed away. They generally held a lot of shares, and their heirs had to pay estate tax.

Valoptec had always favored expansionist strategies. However, at the time, the shareholder base was mostly French. When Essilor went international, Valoptec was unable to follow.

Maintaining your capital ratio is difficult in these conditions. Some of our family-owned rivals chose not to follow international strategies to avoid diluting their capital. In moving overseas, we no longer had total control, but we were the market leaders. They kept control, but had become our followers.

Saint Gobain joined forces with Essilor during this period in two ways. First Saint Gobain was invited to buy Valoptec shares, so we were sure there would be cash to cover thoses wanting to withdraw money. Secondly we asked Saint Gobain to buy Essilor shares so that Saint Gobain and Valoptec would have a controlling share in the company.

Saint Gobain therefore played a key role in the company's governance. We learned a lot during this period and Saint Gobain took part in all our investments.

In the years before 2000, Saint Gobain had the opportunity to make large investments in building materials and distribution, another sector it specialized in. The time came when the stock market asked them to choose between sectors: they chose out. This was a logical decision for them, because the construction sector is much larger than our specialized business, and therefore better suited to Saint Gobain. As Saint Gobain owned nearly 33% of Essilor (worth around 1 billion euros or $1.4 billion, more than we had in equity capital at the time), we needed a solution to replace them.

Around this time, several people suggested we delist Essilor, but that meant putting the company in debt when we needed to invest heavily in Asia (it also would have been the biggest LBO on the Paris market). In any case, competition was too fierce for Essilor to borrow such a huge sum. We chose not to go down this road.

In the end, we bought and subsequently cancelled 7% of the shares, and sold the rest (26%) on the stock exchange. This was a simple and very effective solution. It meant Saint Gobain got their cash and Essilor avoided bringing in new partners. Because the overall number of shares dropped, earnings per share increased. We were in a good financial position to quickly repay the debt we incurred – we managed to pay it back in five years. The only risks we took were not being able to invest heavily for the next three or four years and losing control of the company (our principal shareholder, Valoptec, only had 15% of voting rights). To avoid takeover bids, we aimed for high returns that would make us too expensive for predators. This suggestion came from the financial markets. Our competitive situation was good, so we went for it. After all, if we wanted the freedom that came with this new capital configuration, we had to accept to aim for maximum operational efficiency.

The markets loved it, because we became a pure play – a company with a single business focus and a clear, simple shareholder structure. Six months later, when we posted positive earnings, they rewarded us with a strong increase in capitalization. This made takeover bids even more difficult.

Essilor's management – Philippe Alfroid and I – had pledged to the market we would increase returns. Consequently, for the next three years, we went on a cost-cutting mission that affected the whole company. Essilor had expanded rapidly in the preceding five years as a result of multiple acquisitions in the US, Canada, Australia and New Zealand. It was time to take a break, slow down our acquisitions and take stock of the situation – as we had done in 1990. We needed to pay off our debt as soon as possible. It all went very smoothly.

Philippe and I realized what a powerful tool the financial markets were. We sold our operation to investors at a roadshow, which kicked off in Paris. Our project got a warm welcome in Paris, but in London the following week, it was a major success. We went from one one-to-one meeting – where managers meet investors – to the next. We left knowing the London market was behind us and would invest massively in the operation. At the end of our first day in London, we already had ten times the amount we needed on our books (for market specialists, books are the documents where investors record requests to subscribe to an operation). When you obtain ten times the amount you need in a single afternoon, this is a sure sign the market supports your move. We had 10 billion euros ($13.8 billion) for a company with 3 billion euros ($4.2 billion) capitalization. This was an incredible boost to the project.

The market is therefore a useful tool when you use it carefully and wisely. It helped us come up with the cash for a big block of shares (the day before the operation, Saint Gobain held a 33% stake in Essilor). After this operation, we were well positioned in the financial markets and had a clear outlook. We knew where we were going. We immediately shared this information with Valoptec, our teams and the board, which had given us their total support throughout this delicate period. Then Essilor got back to work.

In other words, before judging the financial market, you must understand what a useful tool it can be to businesses when it is used correctly.

The market economy preceded the stock exchange. The stock exchange only appeared after financial statements were introduced and formulated by the Genoese and Venetians. Nevertheless, it is not a new institution either.

The first transaction records were found in Venice, Genoa, Antwerp and Amsterdam. We know that, with 2,000 ships and 70,000 employees, the Dutch East India Company had a price earnings ratio (the relationship between a company's value and its profits) of 15 during periods of low inflation (almost the same as today). We also know that, at its peak in 1750, the Dutch East India Company had the equivalent of several billion euros in capital and nearly 20,000 shareholders. Listing the company and giving directors the ability to raise funds clearly gave it a competitive advantage over state-owned companies like the Compagnie Française des Indes, despite the support of the French public authorities.

However, the stock exchange does have drawbacks. It has been the scene of many regrettable incidents. One example is the misinformation circulated during the Battle of Waterloo. Financiers knowingly spread false rumors about the outcomes of battles in Paris and London to sway prices in their favor.

In addition, when shares in British railway companies slumped in the 1850s, there were clashes between stockbrokers and the population, which ended with people being hanged. As always, we learn from our errors. As Oscar Wilde said, "Experience is the name everyone gives to their mistakes."

Like all tools, the stock exchange has good and bad sides. The situation has improved significantly. Things still go wrong, but the supervisory authorities are increasingly sophisticated and efficient. In my opinion, the situation has improved every year.

Stop short selling

Currently, all eyes are on the short selling investment technique. It consists in buying shares without actually owning them in anticipation of a drop in value. The idea is simple. Let us say a share is worth $1. You go and see someone who has 100 shares and you borrow them, promising him to give him back 110 in a year's time.

You think the share is going to drop in value. You sell the shares immediately to get the cash. You wait until the share price drops by 50% before buying 110 shares for $55. You return the shares to the person you borrowed them from, and keep the $45 you did not spend. This technique is very profitable if the share price drops over 10%.

However, if the share price rises, your losses can be considerable.

The real ethical issue is when financial analyst firms and brokers – the people in charge of buying and selling on a day-to-day basis – are the ones doing this kind of thing. They have the power to sway share prices by influencing analysts' data and rumors on the market. These practices can (and do) lead to all sorts of abuses, both in the share and the currency exchange markets. Essilor and its shareholders have suffered from this kind of activity several times. Not all short selling operations are dishonest, but we have had several borderline experiences. A company emits extremely favorable recommendations so share prices increase, short sells, and abruptly reverses its recommendations. Its brokers are then ordered to buy up shares, making the company a nice, low-risk profit in the process. In my opinion, this is a scandalous investment technique. Each time we have been targeted by operations like these, we have protested and asked the authorities to look into the situation.

Personally, I think we should stop these activities for five years, and see what happens. Many influential people would no doubt strongly disagree on the basis that this would eliminate a tool that creates market flexibility. My suggestion would therefore be to pass a law requiring short sellers to hold an amount equivalent to three times the short sale in security. By forcing short sellers to invest, excesses could probably be reduced. It would also be possible to carry out trials in one field (in foreign exchange, shares, gold or metals, for example) to test the mechanism. We are certainly not short on ideas. It is my opinion that the authorities need to step in. I am ready to defend the financial markets as a whole, but the excesses of short selling are casting doubt on the profession.

Roadshows, the financial press and how the market works

Short selling aside, the financial market is an excellent tool when managed by ethical people. Most are honest and very hardworking. In the last 20 years, I have had over a thousand one-to-one meetings in major financial centers around the world. I have to admit that the market is a powerful tool, with 35,000 analysts reviewing figures from 35,000 listed companies worldwide and publishing numerous reports.

Brokers (the intermediaries in sales and purchases on the stock exchange) know all the investors and ensure a constant flow of information. Investors who manage portfolios for retirement or insurance funds are extremely competent.

For companies like ours, the markets are an essential part of financial management. We have around 30 investors, whose stakes in Essilor range from 2 to 5%. They know us well, and have worked with us for a long time. Roadshows, twice-yearly meetings where directors present Essilor's figures to the markets, enable us to give everyone the same information at the same time. For management, our investors are a priceless source of information and debate. We know that if we need funds one day, they will be there. When there is a problem, they tell us straight away. Because they have been with us a long time, we are in regular contact and, I am proud to say, we trust many of them implicitly – those who are in it for the long term.

Roadshows are an excellent exercise for directors. Like visits to customers, they are a good way of keeping your feet on the ground.

It is important to be aware of the ways the market can progress, but it is also important to make use of this tool – which can help individuals obtain cash, and companies attract investors or introduce a form of management control. Listing a company does have drawbacks – you must publish your results – but it also results in healthy practices such as constantly controlling costs and calling decisions into question. Unlike our European rivals in ophthalmic optics, we have always been listed. Strangely enough, their strategies have never been bolder than ours.

Even if some investors pull out if they disagree with a new investment, there are always others to take their place. The stock exchange is a vast democracy. I have never heard holders of big funds peddling the infamous "15% annual returns." This figure is mostly thrown around by hedge funds that are heavily in debt. I have always discouraged them from buying shares in Essilor, explaining that we are marathon runners, not sprinters. I tell them that they should not expect miracles with Essilor – our aim is to perform over the long term. We have generally managed to convince them that we are not suited to their strategies. The managers of big funds generally talk about 7% annual returns, the stock exchange's rate of return over 100 years. This is a far cry from the 15% mentioned above.

The market provides valuable services: it sets market prices for shares in large companies, enabling millions of individuals to get involved in this field and giving companies immediate access to cash.

If the stock exchange no longer existed, I am sure the economy would enter into a long depression. We must teach school children about the stock exchange. It would be a fascinating way to start an economics lesson. One Christmas, I gave my nephews small share portfolios. They were amazed. They started reading the economics pages in the paper, and went on to study at excellent business schools.

To conclude, I would like to talk about the financial press and auditors.

The financial press, which I read for long periods of my life, is an intermediary between companies and private investors. In my opinion, it is very professional, and makes every effort to explain stock market figures. It is assisted by auditors, who check the accuracy of independent companies' accounts – their financial discourse, if you will. There was a major scandal in the US around ten years ago when an auditing firm – one of the biggest in the world – just simply disappeared. Auditing accounts is a dangerous business. We should take our hats off to this profession, which goes far beyond simply verifying stock. Auditors are the main guarantors that we can trust the system. Without this trust, the system would not work.

The financial press is careful to report the truth. Spectacular stories are not its priority – although when something spectacular takes place, they do not hold back. There are some remarkable financial journalists who have made a career out of understanding issues without necessarily pointing fingers. With them, you can express yourself freely.

What is more, I think the financial press did an excellent job of covering the financial crisis. They did not hesitate to identify powerful people who had taken wrong turns. The financial press and auditors do society a great service in ensuring accounts are objective.

Shares or SICAVs?

One practical lesson from the current crisis is that we should reduce the number of SICAVs in France.[1] These investment schemes represent a real challenge for small shareholders in terms of transparency. When these shareholders are sold SICAVs, they are told it will help

---

1. Translator's note: a SICAV is a *société d'investissement à capital variable*, an openend mutual fund that invests in short term (one day to one year) debt obligations such as Treasury bills, certificates of deposit, and commercial paper.

them diversify – when really you only need 20 different kinds of shares to diversify. It is much healthier to buy shares in companies you know and whose financial performance you can follow. Companies today have specialized – it is much easier to understand what they do. Private investors do not need a degree in economics to understand ideas such as earnings per share (EPS), price earnings ratio, growth and dividends. There are excellent television programs on the stock market. People are perfectly capable of choosing their own shares. They will have some successes and some failures. It all leads to a better understanding of the economy.

Another French instrument that lacks transparency is the PEA (*plan d'épargne en actions* or share save plan). No one knows what PEAs contain. You are happy when they go up, sad when they go down, but you have no idea why. The stock exchange becomes an unfathomable mystery where "modern and secure" investment instruments inspire suspicion, and have no learning value. Not to mention subprimes, an unfortunate spinoff of SICAVs. Choosing between "dynamic" or "safe" options is a ridiculous exercise. I am in favor of putting an end to these opaque and badly named products.

All shareholders should know what they own and the history of the companies they have invested in. They are all capable of understanding the risks associated with shares, bonds, and securities issued by banks or governments. Banks can and should advise their clients. By investing, each individual should learn more about the economy. In my opinion, it is not good to skip over these subjects – everyone should understand them.

Once again, reason should be the bottom line. Regulate what should be regulated, but know that, without financial markets, the economy would collapse. And I do not know (who does?) what could replace them.

GOOD DEBT:
THE BENETEAU EXAMPLE

"It's risky, Annette, but keep running up debt. With a bit of luck, Beneteau will catch up with Jeanneau in five years, and buy them in ten!"

The experience curve teaches us that market leaders have an advantage over their rivals. Leaders have lower costs and can grow faster, because they have more money.

In theory, if leaders do not make mistakes, they are untouchable. This can be disheartening for followers. Some leaders, who take care to maintain their market share, have dominated their industries for decades.

Fortunately, however, things are not always so simple. Theory and practice are two different things. Real life cannot be learned at school, and experience is gained in the field. Life has its ups and downs. Mindset and willpower have a lot to do with it. In business, nothing is impossible!

The best competitive upset I ever experienced was the battle between Beneteau and Jeanneau from 1970 to 1982.

I met Beneteau's directors, Annette and Louis-Claude Roux, in 1976. I initially worked with them as a consultant for BCG and later joined the group as managing director. It was an unforgettable experience. I come from a family of doctors, lawyers, naval officers, politicians and clergymen. In other words, I was not really destined for the business world. BCG let me spread my wings, but it was at Beneteau that I really took off, thanks to some excellent mentors.

In 1976, Beneteau was one of the top ten pleasure boat producers. At the time, the leader of this very young industry was Jeanneau. Jeanneau's lead over its rivals was considerable, and its turnover was 80 million Francs ($17.3 million). Dufour was Jeanneau's closest competitor and Beneteau, with turnover of 30 million Francs ($6.5 million), was in fifth position. Because Beneteau was less than half the size of Jeanneau, it was in a seemingly precarious position. However, Beneteau managed to make some impressive waves. Here's how.

Beneteau took advantage of the rapidly expanding market to grow faster than its competitors, including Jeanneau.

First, a little bit of history. The French love affair with sailing began with Eric Tabarly, who managed to win over Charles de Gaulle. Georges Pompidou, France's president at the time, encouraged the construction of ultramodern ports that were envied by the rest of Europe. The French pleasure boating market grew 15% per year. And within this market, the shift from wood to plastic meant fiberglass boat sales grew by 25% per year.

In a stagnant market, it is difficult for followers to grow, because whatever they win in market share, the leader loses. The leader hits back, and has a higher strike force than its rivals. However, in a rapidly expanding market, competitors can grow faster than the leader without the leader actually realizing it. Because the leader is also growing, it is under the impression it is maintaining and even reinforcing its market position.

Market share is "sticky" in slow growing industries, but more fluid in fast growing ones. In a market that is growing 25% per year, market share is completely fluid.

Jeanneau's major problem was, surprisingly, its principal shareholder. Jeanneau was a subsidiary of an American group, Bangor Punta, known for Piper aircraft. In theory, Jeanneau had the financial backing of this big group, which made the situation harder for its followers who were essentially just successful SMEs. In practice, however, Bangor Punta had focused all its attention on Piper aircraft and pumped Jeanneau for dividends equal to 60% of profits.[1]

---

1. See Appendices, T 6.

Jeanneau had the perfect profile for a market leader. It had no debts. It showed its power by paying out big dividends. However, this meant it was unable to fully take advantage of the booming market.

Meanwhile, Beneteau did the reverse. It paid out no dividends at all, and reinvested all its profits. In addition, for every Franc reinvested, it borrowed an additional Franc.

I remember perfectly my first conversation with Annette Roux. She was concerned about Jeanneau's apparent force. I immediately told her that Jeanneau's strength was actually a weakness in a rapidly expanding market. Beneteau's apparent weakness was a major advantage if it was put to good use. That was all the reassurance Annette needed: her willpower and daring did the rest.

The strength of the competitors made me say to her, "It's risky, but keep running up debt. With a bit of luck, you'll catch up with Jeanneau in five years, and buy them in ten!" She replied, "You're on!" A short time later, I joined Beneteau.

This story is an excellent example of when running up strategic debt works. It is therefore worth going into more detail. Beneteau's debt is a far cry from the unsustainable borrowings that caused recent events – where wealth was transferred to shareholders to the detriment of the company.

Financing growth

The table in Appendices T 6 presents simple financial data from both companies demonstrating their different financial policies in 1976. At the time, Jeanneau earned 80 million Francs ($17.3 million) and Beneteau 30 million ($6.5 million).

Jeanneau made 12.2 million Francs ($2.6 million) in profits, and paid 4.3 million ($930,000) in taxes. After paying out dividends of 4.7 million Francs or $1,000,200 (60% of 7.9 million Francs or $1,670,000), it had 3.2 million ($669,800) left to invest. As the company had assets worth 41 million Francs ($8.9 million), this theoretically resulted in 8% growth (3.2 divided by 41).[2]

---

2. See Appendices, T 6.

Beneteau's profits after financial charges were 5.5 million Francs ($1,190,000 million). After paying 1.9 million in taxes ($411,000), it had 3.6 million ($779,000) remaining. Beneteau paid no dividends and borrowed 1 Franc for every Franc reinvested – 3.6 million Francs ($779,000).

Beneteau therefore invested 7.2 million Francs ($1,558,000), double Jeanneau's sum, despite being less than half the size of than the market leader. The company's theoretical growth rate was 50% (7.2 divided by 14).

Beneteau caught up to Jeanneau in 1981-82, when both companies had turnover of 170 million Francs ($36.8 million). Jeanneau's annual growth was 12%, while Beneteau's was 40%. Jeanneau never even saw Beneteau coming.

Beneteau's perfectly executed strategy also relied on another clever tactic. In those days, Jeanneau built sailboats and motorboats, while Beneteau specialized in sailboats. My arrival at Beneteau was heralded as a sign that the company was moving into motorboats. Jeanneau therefore invested in motorboats to circumvent this expansion. However, it was a ruse! Jeanneau's investments were useless, and Beneteau overtook Jeanneau in sailboats.

In the early 1970s, Beneteau's costs were higher than Jeanneau's because it had less experience and higher financial charges (because of its debt). It still managed to travel down the experience curve more quickly. The two companies' profit curves intersected. And, obviously, from 1981 onwards, Beneteau's costs were lower than Jeanneau's.

When this crucial period had passed, it was no longer necessary for Beneteau to run up debt. Its loans were a risk if the market dropped for any reason. Annette Roux decided to sell some of Beneteau's capital on the stock market and use the money to pay off the company's debt. This is not common practice for companies entering the stock exchange. Beneteau could have finished Jeanneau off.

However, Jeanneau was spared the death knell, because Beneteau began having osmosis problems in the hulls of some boats. This slowed activity at the boatyards for five years. Fortunately, the group was no longer in debt. If it had been, the consequences would have been disastrous.

At this point, Jeanneau's senior management – encouraged by private equity funds (already making their mark) – decided to take control of the company as part of a LMBO. Unfortunately, they leveraged the company too heavily for the operation to be successful. They were up to their necks in debt while Beneteau was resolving its technical problems. The rest of the story was short but sweet: Jeanneau collapsed, and Beneteau bought them out. A global leader was born.

With its trials and tribulations, this story illustrates the positive sides to strategic debt, but also the qualities required of a good CEO: daring, persistence, prudence and excellent timing.

EMPLOYEE SHAREHOLDERS

Becoming employee shareholders

I remember attending one of Valoptec's general assemblies just after Saint Gobain sold its stake in Essilor. As employee shareholders, we all understood the need to rally together. I was approached by a retired foreman who had worked with us all his life. He had accumulated a nice little nest egg (you will get an idea of what this amounts to below) because he had never sold any of his shares. He asked me if he could sell some shares to help his daughter, who had just got married, buy a house. He was worried about the effect this would have on our control over the company. The foreman's attitude was remarkable, because he was retired and no longer had any reason to worry about Essilor. Naturally I told him that he should take advantage of this money – he deserved it after so many years of faithful service. But he understood our situation. Instinctively, he knew that the capital he owned was not just money, it was also power over Essilor. It was power over the company and its unique corporate spirit, and he did not want to give it up without my agreement. Employee shareholders (even retired) are more responsible than other shareholders. In making it possible to implement lasting strategies and management practices, they ensure the company spirit remains intact. This is why work and capital should go together. It is much more than a question of money.

Countries with good quality of life are generally those where people get satisfaction from what they do. This means that individuals feel that their work, or the risks they take as business owners, are worth what they get paid. However, it also means they feel they have some degree of control over their destiny. If these conditions are met, society is likely to be harmonious. We can learn a lot from employee shareholding.

If we want a system that withstands the test of time, we must focus not only on sharing but also on creating wealth. Sharing wealth in such a way as to discourage its creation is a bad idea. Unfortunately, this is often the case. In addition, if those who create wealth are not fair in sharing it, employee motivation will drop and operational efficiency will suffer. Employee shareholding is a simple solution to both problems.

Back to company basics

For centuries, companies have operated by the same simple rules: shareholders take risks, and employees are paid salaries, whether the company makes a profit or not. The shareholder bears any losses and has the right to profits – when there are any. Because shareholders have a right to the profits, they decide how these sums are divided between dividends and reinvestment.

The idea to give employees a share in profits is not new. In France, Charles de Gaulle was the first to make this official 40 years ago by passing a law on employee shareholding. France's current president Nicolas Sarkozy recently raised the topic again with his "three thirds" idea.

"For a long time now I've thought the three thirds rule was a good rule. If profit is 100, 33 should go to employees, 33 directly to shareholders and 33 reinvested in the company," he said.

The advantage of this rule is that it is clear and simple, and the underlying idea is commendable. Unfortunately, reality is much more complex and, if applied in this form, the rule could give rise to serious economic distortions.

In my opinion, it is impossible to establish a simple ratio for distributing profits. Each company has its own business model, which requires more or less investment, and the situation changes from year to year. A simple rule would overlook how complex the economy is and how it changes over time. It is also good for companies to decide how they allocate their resources, especially given the changing international environment.

The extraordinary complexity of the economy

We do not always realize that there is such an incredible variety of companies making up modern economies. Their characteristics are as varied as those of different flora and fauna (see A Short Guide to Economics III).

A catering company requires very little or no capital, because it gets paid by customers before it pays suppliers. A ski-lift company, however, require investments equal to three times its turnover. Both companies' division of capital and labor is completely different. For the first company, labor represents 95% of value-added and there is almost no need for capital – the company does not need its third. The second company requires a great deal of capital so more than one third must be reinvested.

The choice between dividends and investment varies depending on company growth. When the company is expanding early on in the life cycle, 100% of profits must be reinvested. In financial terms, the company's retention rate is 100%. When the company consolidates its competitive position and market growth slows (a sign that the market is maturing), it can pay dividends of around 20%. Only when market growth drops to 1 or 2% can dividends increase – as long as companies take care not to lose market share, which would affect profits. These decisions require perspicacity and diplomacy.

In reality, these variables (capital intensity, market share and growth) combine to produce a great variety of situations. Consequently, establishing fixed ratios for the division of wealth between labor, investment and dividends would lead to serious economic distortions. Too much would be invested in some areas, and not enough in others. Too much would be paid in dividends when it was inappropriate or even hazardous to do so, and not enough when the time was right. In addition, as companies become increasingly global, it is inappropriate to treat employees from one country differently to those of other nationalities.

If we introduce the rule of three thirds, capital, already subject to competitive constraints, will also be subject to legal constraints. Investors will flee to other countries. Obviously, in the current context, this is not the best option.

Employee shareholding

Contrary to popular belief, capital and labor are allies and depend on each other. Without investors to provide money, there are no machines, no products, no companies and no jobs. Similarly, capital clearly cannot prosper without employees. The question is therefore how to build a harmonious relationship between the two.

There is an extremely simple solution, which allows wealth to be shared with employees while encouraging wealth creation through increased motivation. This solution is employee shareholding.

This does not mean arbitrarily deciding that companies must give part of their profits to employees. This would be unfair to existing shareholders and, if we are not careful, could result in a form of the rule of three thirds.

The aim is to help those companies wishing to give their employees shares in capital find a fair, long-term solution. Under French law, they can do this in three ways: through savings schemes, performance shares and stock options. The tools are there, we just need to use them.

Employee shareholders and capital

If the company is successful in the long term, holding shares can allow employees to accumulate considerable capital over their lifetime.

Let us take the example of a worker who joined Essilor 41 years ago. If they paid 7% of their salary into our savings scheme every month, they would have 600,000 euros ($850,000) by the time they retired. A foreman is capable of making double! In both situations, these sums are over twice the minimum pension paid out by the French government. However, 7% is a considerable amount to pay out every month, and employees have to trust their employers. It is true that Essilor's shares have done extremely well, and Essilor matches contributions made by employees in savings schemes. We are one of the more generous employers. However, statistics show that these schemes also have good results in "traditional" companies.

For example, let us take a company with 7% average return on capital in the long term. An employee who deposits 7% of her salary with the company making matching contributions ultimately saves

200,000 euros ($283,000). Even if she only deposits 3.5% of her salary, this still amounts to 100,000 euros ($142,000). In both situations, the employee wins.

Governance

Money is one aspect of employee shareholding. It is an important aspect, but not the only one. Another aspect is employees' participation in corporate governance. For those with longstanding schemes, this is one of the main benefits of the system.

When employees have shares in a company, they join the board of directors. The number of seats is calculated on a pro rata basis in line with the number of shares. These representatives sit alongside independent board members, and have their say in company matters. This gives them a clear idea of the company's different activities. This is a rewarding experience that they can share with their colleagues. Experience shows that it also ensures better understanding, communication and involvement of and in important decisions.

At Essilor, communication with employee shareholders is managed by Valoptec. Valoptec organizes monthly meetings between management and employee representatives. Every six months, it also organizes general assemblies where decisions are made by secret ballot. This includes resolutions and HR policy and strategy.

Many companies have implemented similar schemes. They can attest to the fact that the atmosphere changes when staff hold shares and take part in governance activities. The management team, guided by the board of directors, has the final say on decisions, but it also answers to employee shareholders. When employees hold shares and act like shareholders, their relationship to the company is completely different than it would be in traditional structures.

When the group has had a difficult year, and the management team must ask employees for extra efforts, decisions on regional and sector-specific (sales, production and R&D) contributions are made in an afternoon. This is remarkable for a global group. People know that, to look after their money, the company must sometimes cut back.

However, the most impressive thing about shareholding is the dignity and responsibility it confers on the employees concerned.

To this very day, I remember announcing to our Indian employees that they could hold shares in the company. They got up on tables and gave us a standing ovation, which lasted for five minutes. The next day, we visited different offices to film our employees' reactions. Basically, they said, they felt like they were at home. Allowing them to hold shares gave them a whole new way of looking at Essilor. They had acquired the status of owners, and could henceforth influence corporate strategy.

We did the same thing in China, after the Chinese government authorized us to introduce employee shareholding. The government understood the benefits of the operation, which it watches over benevolently. We were all pleased to see Mr. He Yi, head of our Chinese operations, become Essilor board member – one of the three representatives of Essilor employees at the board.

Taking the plunge

However, things are not always simple. Employee shareholding takes a lot of commitment. Not everyone wants to invest more in the company. Shares can go up, but they can also go down. You need people with a stomach for it. In exchange for their commitment, employee shareholders know that the best returns come from day-to-day performance and long service. This is essential in terms of motivation.

The Essilor team has always been exemplary in this respect. Despite the company's solid overall performance, Essilor shares have been volatile on two occasions: in 1990, when the group decided to focus on lenses; and again during the recent financial crisis. On both occasions, our employee shareholders refused to sell. They have unfailingly supported management whenever serious decisions had to be made, even though these decisions affected some of them directly.

When we needed to take risks, they were always there. It took daring to invest heavily in the US in 1996. Some players on the stock market considered our operations would be less profitable and pulled out of Essilor. The Essilor team stood strong, and those who doubted us bitterly regret their actions today.

Obviously, as Essilor's chairman, I promote employee shareholding to politicians. I am a strong supporter of stock options and performance shares, which are some of the best ways of encouraging this involvement – when they are implemented correctly. At Essilor, employee shareholding is governed by strict but simple rules. Firstly, these rewards do not dilute existing capital, because the shares issued (between 0.8 and 1% per year) are bought up and cancelled in the year. Secondly, around 8,000 employees take part in the scheme each year. Senior management also has shares in the company, but in reasonable proportions (3 to 4% of the total – or 10 to 20 times less than the percentages that recently shocked the general public). Senior management (the CEO and COO) generally reinvest capital gains on stock options in Essilor. Their shares are more than half of what they own, and they act like individual entrepreneurs.

French legislation on employee shareholders

French law on employee shareholder authorizes matching contributions by companies. Employers can therefore double the first 5,000 euros ($7,090) invested by employees. Up to a set limit, employees can also buy shares at prices 20% below the listed price. These two options create opportunities for employees: the initial sums invested by employees are immediately multiplied by 2.5. For example, you choose to invest $5,000 a year. Essilor matches your $5,000, bringing your total investment to $10,000. You decide to purchase Essilor shares. Because you are able to purchase them 20% below the market price, you end up with $12,500. Because the law creates such favorable conditions, Essilor insists on employees assuming the risks of their actions.

Nevertheless, employee shareholding is still regarded with suspicion. People say, "You're putting all your eggs in one basket! If things go badly, you lose both labor and capital." We consider the profits made by shareholders are justified… by the risks they take. Profits make taking risks worthwhile – and that is where employee shareholders come in. After all, we are free to choose not to take risks, but that means forgetting about sharing profit.

Employee shareholding schemes are not as common as they should be in France. But I believe that, in time, they will be.

Long service and fidelity

As our principal shareholders, Essilor employees hold around 14% of voting rights at the time of writing. They are also our most legitimate shareholders, because they have been with us since the beginning, and they stick with us during the hard times. Even if they no longer hold a majority share, they ensure the group remains consistent and faithful to its objectives.

Without its employee shareholders and faithful pensioners, the group might have been bought by investment funds that would have pumped it dry. The company would have lost its soul, and would never have become as large as it is today, because people would not be as committed as they are now. The company would not have made the daring investments it has made. It is thanks to our employee shareholders – their motivation, the support they give to the management team (there have been four CEOs in 40 years), and the time they give us to act in – that our working environment is so good and the company has been so successful. This is why we reward loyalty.

However, we run up against another obstacle: the financial market itself.

Currently, the market is not in favor of rewarding loyal shareholders by doubling their voting rights or increasing their dividends. Whenever we raise this idea at our general assemblies, it is voted down.

Nevertheless, loyalty should be rewarded in one form or another because it allows the company to grow. You cannot develop long-term strategies if you fear losing investors. I support the free flow of capital – the stock market is an excellent invention, precisely because it is flexible. This flexibility, and the ease with which we buy and sell shares, is what makes it possible to match up supply of capital with demand for investment. However, flexibility is not incompatible with rewarding loyalty. It is a question of finding a happy medium.

Doubling voting rights and dividends for those who have held shares for over five years is a small shift in power and money which would do a great deal of good. It is impossible to implement long-term strategies with shareholders who are primarily focused on the short-term.

The public sector could encourage long-term shareholding by exempting these shareholders from taxes (such as capital gains or wealth taxes). This would be a strong signal in favor of employee shareholding schemes and sharing added value. It would reinforce company leadership.

Encouraging ownership

Men and women from all walks of life should benefit from the fruits of their labor. This means setting aside money or making investments, no matter how small.

Not recognizing this simple reality is an attack on personal dignity. Ownership, even on a small scale, confers dignity and creates a sense of safety.

When you own nothing and live from hand to mouth, it is difficult to take even the smallest risk. One of the best things about ownership is that it encourages daring.

Taking risks is essential for personal development. People with property find it much easier to be flexible – a necessary quality in today's society. They no longer fear change, but are confident in the future.

Ownership is the best way to build trust.

"EMPLOYEE SHAREHOLDERS
CAN MAKE A DIFFERENCE"

Aicha Mokdahi, chairman of Valoptec, Essilor's employee shareholder association, talks about Valoptec's role in day-to-day activities and the group's long-term success.

LAURENT ACHARIAN – *How does Valoptec work?*

AICHA MOKDAHI – We have a board of directors with 16 members who represent different employee categories and retirees. Of these members, eight represent different categories (supervisors, managers and retirees) and the rest represent regions (the US, Canada, Europe and Asia). The board nominates a chairman, who must be based in the Paris region to be close to the group's general management team. Today, Valoptec is becoming more international in scope, and represents an increasing number of retired staff. Nine percent of retired employees now hold 52 percent of Essilor's employee shareholding. This goes to show how retired employees show their trust in the group by leaving their savings intact and taking part in the decision-making process.

What role does Valoptec play in the company?

Valoptec is Essilor's principal shareholder. Consequently, 5,000 of Essilor's 34,000 employees hold 6.2% of the company's capital and 14% of voting rights. No strategic decisions can be made without consulting us or obtaining our approval.

We intervene in different ways. Three of Valoptec's board members also sit on Essilor's board of directors. The first Chinese administrator of a CAC 40 company obtained this role thanks to Valoptec. It's also thanks to Valoptec that another woman – me – joined the board of directors.

Valoptec's board of directors meets every two months. At each meeting, Hubert Sagnières, Essilor's COO, gives us a presentation on Essilor's progress and strategy, the acquisitions underway and other important subjects.

Valoptec also holds a general assembly every six months. It's at these meetings that, once a year, we hold a vote of confidence in the company's general management (a vote on company strategy and HR policies). We also vote on the resolutions that will be voted on at Essilor's annual general assembly. Everyone votes using an electronic voting machine and the results only take 30 seconds.

What impact does Valoptec have on corporate governance?

Employee shareholders are stakeholders in the group's governance structures. This helps them trust and take responsibility for the company's progress.

This plays a determining role in staff behavior. There's a joke at Essilor that goes along the lines of, "How can you tell if someone is a member of Valoptec? They turn the light off when they leave the office."

Valoptec's members have the ability to take action. They're involved in the decision-making process, and push the general management team to explain their actions. This was the case last March, for example, when the group wanted to acquire FGX International, even though their main activity isn't ophthalmic optics. We work in partnership with managers, and look out for the company's interests.

What role do you play with respect to trade unions?

We have complementary roles. Valoptec is concerned with the company's longevity and growth. We're there to make things run smoothly. We defend the interests of employee shareholders. We always prefer discussion to confrontation. But that doesn't mean we can't make ourselves heard. For example, Valoptec successfully prevented the closure of a subsidiary and production plant. We're all about dialogue, that's what builds trust.

How do employees gain from holding shares?

Over the last few years, I can't think of a better way for Essilor employees to invest money than by taking part in the employee shareholding scheme. Let me give you an example. One of my colleagues told me he bought a house in the Paris region in 2000. He also had shares in Essilor for the last 20 years. Between the increase in share value on the stock market and the company's matched contributions, he multiplied his initial investment by five. Some supervisors even own several houses thanks to this system, which helps them build up their retirement.

Employees can invest up to 25% of their salary in Valoptec. Many of them contribute considerable sums every month.

Is this the way of the future?

We regularly get asked this question by other large companies, but I think the system is difficult to imitate. This model is the result of our history as a workers' cooperative.

In any case, the model has a bright future at Essilor, because the new managing director wants Valoptec to have 20% of voting rights, compared to 14% today. He understands that it's the best way of encouraging employee involvement, protecting company capital and ensuring the model is passed down to future generations. It's what makes Essilor unique.

PART V

A COMPETITIVE NATION

"DON'T DO IT, MY SON!"

Risky capital

Traditionally, MEDEF's chairman holds regular meetings with philosophers, religious authorities, artists and intellectuals.[1] It is one of the organization's customs.

Ernest-Antoine Seillière, MEDEF's former chairman, invited me to take part in episcopal conferences several times. Generally, this meeting was a dinner with no set program. Our discussions were always lively and extremely interesting.

We usually picked over current events while having a drink before dinner. Once debate was underway, it always took unexpected turns. This was extremely enlightening for us businessmen.

No matter what some of its (more left-leaning) members say, the Catholic Church contributed to ideas that later formed the basis of the market economy by underlining what is divine in each individual. Each individual has a unique genius that enables him to take responsibility and make decisions.

It is not by chance that Europe, the world's first Christian stronghold, is where the market economy originated. In this region, individual initiatives were encouraged. Confucianism, on the other hand, had a different view of human beings. It attributed more importance to

---

1. Translator's note: MEDEF (the *Mouvement des Entreprises de France* or Movement of French Enterprises) is France's largest union of employers.

obedience, tradition and the state, as incarnated by the Emperor. In regions influenced by this philosophy, the market economy developed much later.

I approve of and enjoy contact with our French bishops. I was always happy to take part in these meetings.

One evening, conversation was slow to get going, despite the fact we had all met each other before. Ernest-Antoine was in an excellent mood, but nothing could lighten the atmosphere. The bishops had something on their minds.

The dinner put on by MEDEF was not at all lavish, so that was obviously not the problem.

I even started wondering whether there was some serious problem they could not tell us about. After 15 minutes, I asked them what subjects they had had to deal with that day.

A bishop said, "Mr. Fontanet, we worked on the question of poverty all day long. Why are there so many poor people in France? The problem is gaining momentum at the moment, you must have noticed."

So that was it. "It's a serious issue that affects all of us, and it's something that concerns businessmen as well," I replied.

I understood why the bishops had been preoccupied, but I did not know how to explain my point of view. Then I had an idea. Knowing Ernest-Antoine's sense of humor, I said to him, "Ernest-Antoine, what you need to do is sell all your businesses and give all the proceeds to the Church. You won't regret it on Judgment Day!"

His reply went something like this: "What a great idea, Xavier! Good timing too, I was getting sick of working all the time. I want to spend more time with my family. But there's a slight problem: if I close down, 40,000 people will lose their jobs!"

"Don't do it, my son!" exclaimed one of bishops.

I was surprised by the "my son" and the vehemence of his tone.

The evening had begun!

This spontaneous reaction was very welcome to the businessmen present. It was an encouragement that meant a lot to us. He was basically saying, "Don't get rid of the wealth that keeps other people employed. This wealth is valuable to society as a whole. If there are such things as good and bad wealth, businessmen who set up companies and create jobs are examples of good wealth."

If you think about it, the economy is based on sales – trade between two free people. When you realize this, your perception of the market changes radically. Companies only exist to make trade possible. In some ways, they are its servants.

Making a profit is now considered a bad thing, to the point that we can no longer talk about it objectively. But if we do not seek to understand it – to know when profit is good or bad – we will be unable to live together harmoniously. We will pass up an extraordinary opportunity: opening up to the world.

Profit can be described as what companies get in return for providing a service. Profit is the reward customers give suppliers.

Consequently, a company's capitalization (estimating its future profits, determining the stock market value of these profits, determining the sum it costs to buy the company and evaluating the value of its owners' capital) just measures the service provided to customers worldwide.

Bill Gates is not the richest man in the world because he was the best at exploiting computer programmers. He is the richest man in the world because he developed the Windows operating system and knew how to market it around the world. This system has changed the way people around the world interact.

It is because of Bill Gates that we have the computer programs we use daily. It is because of him that we communicate by email. This IT revolution is only rivaled by the invention of the printing press. The fact that he made his fortune and created a charity in the process is a good thing. But he did a lot more good by setting up a company that spread around the world.

The same can be said of most listed companies. Capitalization just measures the value of services rendered. Capital can also be considered in another way. Capital creates jobs. This is what led the bishop to say, "Don't do it, my son!"

As time goes by, businesses become more capital dependent. They require machines, stock and working capital. This is a natural consequence of progress, increased production levels and technology. It is also what drives prices and costs down, and sales up. A company cannot operate, much less grow, without capital.

Many French people are unaware that labor is dependent on capital. The word "capital" has negative connotations. We do not think enough about it.

Did you know, for example, that each job at Essilor requires a 300,000 euro ($422,000) investment in capital? We use extremely complex machinery, and our lenses are the result of considerable expertise – IT strength. Our lenses require enormous computers and complex supply chains. Every day, we monitor millions of lenses, many of which are tailor made. These lenses pass through hundreds of factories and warehouses. People are too quick to forget that entrepreneurs invest in capital to finance jobs.

People also forget that there is no such thing as a guaranteed return on capital in today's competitive world.

No one decides to risk their capital lightly.

If nobody was willing to risk money (in other words, if nobody was willing to lose money if they invested badly), employment would drop significantly. This is something everyone agrees on, but we need reminding of. In some ways, taking risks is what owning capital is all about. This is what the Parable of the Talents (in the Gospel) is all about. It should be renamed the investment or entrepreneur parable.

Leon XIII or Jean-Paul II (in the encyclicals *Rerum Novarum* and *Centesimus Annus* respectively) are both strong defenders of the market economy, as long as it serves mankind. They understand that competition ensures the market serves consumers. Competition is necessary to prevent monopolies, where producers dominate customers and free trade is no longer possible.

The welfare state and poverty

Poverty is an extremely sensitive and painful subject, which can only be discussed with care and discretion. Especially when you are a businessman and earn a better living than many. However, business owners should give their opinions on this subject.

My conversation with the bishops shed new light on the subject. The wealth that is risked in business is not responsible for poverty. It alleviates poverty because it creates jobs.

Rich societies must set aside money for those who are less fortunate. There is no doubt about that. It is up to politicians to decide how much. The sum might change, but not the underlying principle. That is what entrepreneurs believe.

We also believe that politicians must be careful to not go too far. In other words, they must avoid creating situations of dependency where able-bodied people are dissuaded from actively looking for work because of excessive benefit payments. Care should be taken to ensure benefit payments do not create distortions that upset the balance of society, like the famous "unemployment trap." Why go to work in a factory when the government pays you the same amount to stay at home?

In France, we have already fallen into this trap. Other countries pay welfare, for example, but ask beneficiaries to carry out tasks for the public good in exchange.

If companies do not create poverty, who does?

And what if the culprit was… the government? A government that is too unproductive, levies too many taxes, and redistributes too much income. French companies pay too many taxes and social security contributions. Because of this, they have trouble exporting. As a member of a global company, I can safely say that taxes and transfers are higher in France than anywhere else in the world. And who suffers? The people we cannot afford to hire.

This is the problem with the welfare state. In France a majority of people believe that the state's money is heaven-sent. They forget this money comes from taxes. They forget that the money the state is spending is actually theirs! Another example of the danger in twisting words.

If you read the encyclicals carefully, the popes have always adopted a cautious approach to the welfare state. This is especially true of Jean-Paul II, who had firsthand experience of a state that wanted to control everything. A state that wanted to do good, but that ended up creating systems that destroyed individual initiative and society itself.

My conversation with the bishops took place several years ago. The welfare state is an impossible dream. It seems as if we may finally be waking up to this fact.

ALAIN JUPPÉ

"Xavier, you defend individual interests. I defend the public interest."

Seven or eight years ago, I was invited to present at a conference organized by MEDEF. French prime minister Alain Juppé was the guest of honor.

I gave an overview of Essilor's history to illustrate the group's international focus. I then told the audience that I was surprised that French entrepreneurs were not considered generous, because companies created real wealth.

I explained my theory for this. Businessmen make the tactical mistake of talking too much about profits, performance and market share and not enough about the human side of entreprise. Because of this focus on economics, French people consider businessmen are not interested in people. So in France, performance and generosity began to be seen as mutually exclusive. Another French exception!

I then explained that, to fill the gap, other entities had taken on this role.

This vacuum has been filled by politicians. In France, the state and politicians have appropriated the fields of "generosity" and "assistance." They scrupulously avoid mentioning the businesses that make this benevolence possible. And, to take the cake, they distribute money that is not actually "theirs," as they claim it is, but "ours." This money belongs to companies, but also taxpayers. There are not many countries in the world where this fiction prevails. Generally, people talk about taxpayer money. In Great Britain and the United States, for example, the government puts "your taxes at work" on signs warning of road works.

Left-wing politicians in France are even more cunning, because they have fully appropriated anything to do with the heart.

I finished my speech by telling the audience about a discussion I had with my youngest daughter on the important subjects of freedom and fraternity.

"Last month, I was talking to my daughter Caroline, who is finishing engineering school.

She asked me, 'Dad, why do company directors like you have such a bad reputation? I know you and your friends, who are also company directors. You're normal people, what's happening?'

I said to her, 'I think it's a bit over the top too. Some people do bad things, but we're not like them. I don't think it's fair to blame all company directors.'

'That said, maybe our problem is communication. We might be too idealistic in our demands. For example, we ask the government to reduce bureaucracy and protect entrepreneurial freedom. We do this because we think it's the key to individual initiative. We think that when you're free to take the initiative, the economy is so dynamic everyone (employers and employees) benefits. State intervention to redistribute wealth is no longer necessary. We don't ask the state to redistribute wealth, maybe that's why we're not considered generous.'

'If I put it another way, I don't think it's up to the state or the government to give children chocolate at school, for example. That doesn't mean I disagree with children eating chocolate. It's just that, if the state hands out chocolate, it has to collect taxes beforehand. I'd prefer parents paid fewer taxes and gave the chocolate to their children themselves. I know that if there were fewer obstacles in the way of business initiatives in France, and if the state was less expensive, the economy would be much more robust and all the children would get chocolate.'

'Caroline, if I keep working hard for Essilor and MEDEF, it's because I want to develop these ideas, bring the public and private sectors closer together, and leave my children a good country to live in.'"

The company directors in the audience applauded this speech enthusiastically.

At the cocktail that followed the conference, I was approached by Alain Juppé. He was interested in Essilor, and perhaps taken aback by the audience's reaction to my speech.

"Xavier, it's great what you're doing at Essilor, but you only defend individual interests. That's easy. I defend the public interest. It's much more difficult."

I must admit, I was flabbergasted. It had never crossed my mind that, in the course of my work, I "only defended individual interests." My main preoccupation is ensuring there is a good working environment. I know that it depends on a good strategy and paying attention to people. My concerns are our customers, our accounts, our acquisitions and joint ventures and the law. All the rest is just a reward: the enjoyment that comes with working as part of a good team, the company's good reputation, feeling useful, the satisfaction of our investors and our share price on the stock market.

I was both surprised and worried, because I did not understand his remark straight away. I was so taken aback I do not even remember what I replied. It cannot have had much of an impact. But I thought long and hard about what he said.

Competition and individual interests: Swiss and Japanese watches

In some ways it is true that Essilor defends individual interests: those of our shareholders. But I do not think we do this to the detriment of the public interest, because competition keeps us in check. Mr. Juppé was right in some ways, but he overlooked the fact that we work in a competitive environment. This is no trivial matter.

In France, we like competition when it is on the soccer field or at the supermarket – when it is a means of comparison. We do not like it when it applies to us as employees or is used to call us into question.

In the United States, competition is essential to all decision-making. It is naturally considered a good thing that creates social mobility. It is another form of freedom. In Japan, where there are few natural resources, they know they are surrounded by giants. From a very young age, Japanese children learn that they must do better than their competitors on the international markets to survive. This is not the case in France, where competition means stress and the survival of the fittest. Competition is seen as an unacceptable source of inequality.

However, competition has many hidden virtues that work to our advantage without our knowledge.

Take the watch industry, for example. Since the Lip affair,[1] France has withdrawn completely from this industry and the French are no longer involved in watches. Nevertheless, everyone agrees that this industry has made a lot of progress – whether for top of the line or everyday watches. In the latter market, which concerns most of us, prices have quite literally collapsed. Today, a watch that costs $30 is more reliable than the most expensive watches sold 20 years ago. Most watches are water-resistant. Since Lip's withdrawal from this industry, French consumers have also benefitted from these developments. We did not contribute directly to the process, but we did, however, contribute by exercising our rights as consumers each time we bought new watches.

It was because of the market mechanism that we were all able to benefit from an industry we divested!

Where did these continual improvements come from if not the competition opposing Swiss and Japanese watchmakers over the last 30 years? Because of competition, consumers benefitted from technological progress almost immediately. They only had to shop around.

Competitors must be constantly on the lookout. Customers are only loyal to a certain point, after that you must reduce costs, increase innovation and produce at lower prices. In our lifetimes, we are all producers and consumers. The disadvantages of being a producer are offset by the benefits of being a consumer.

Japanese watchmakers might defend individual interests, but they are also held in check by their Swiss competitors and consumer demands. These two factors ensure that individual interests respect other interests.

Of course, we can always dream of societies where everyone works for the public good, where there is no competition and there are no individual interests. But, as we know, even the best-laid plans go

---

1. Translator's note: LIP is a French watch and clock company. After the company experienced financial problems in the 1960s and 1970s, workers went on strike and occupied the factory. The company later went into liquidation.

awry – past experience has shown us this. In the meantime, we have to admit that competition and individual interests work together to create a happy medium. Competition checks individual interests and ensures they are also in the public interest.

Monopolies and the public interest

Sometimes states create monopolies over services, on the basis that this is in the public interest. Decisions like this should never be taken lightly, because they are difficult to reverse and have an impact on resource allocation.

Indeed, public goods are provided at zero cost to consumers. They are paid for by taxes, levied once a year. Their overall cost is not individualized – it is just one lump sum.

All competition is immediately eliminated (who can survive with no turnover?). Consumers cannot control quality by switching to competitors. Their only option is to show their overall satisfaction or dissatisfaction by voting in general elections.

This is obviously the only solution when it comes to law and order (the justice system, police, foreign affairs and local authorities). Similar systems are at work all around the world – the first nations were created as a result of grouping these functions. However, food, housing, clothing, entertainment and other needs have all been relegated to the private sector. It is extremely rare for them to come under public control. Between these two extremes are services (such as education, health and transport) that can be public or private, depending on the country.

When the public sector takes over a service, it immediately benefits from national economies of scale. It avoids the segmentation caused by different customer groups. However, it loses control of costs, which can lead to large deficits. Competition no longer keeps the service provider on its toes. And the public sector cannot take advantage of global economies of scale. This phenomenon has been observed, for example, in France's public health insurance system (see Bastiat's text on supplementary health insurance[2]). The public sector is at a disadvantage, because the private sector operates internationally.

---

2. See Bastiat's text, "Mutual aid societies" (Appendices).

Realistically, globalization means reconsidering the division of tasks between the public and private sectors.

The real risk for society is that these organizations come to serve their employees rather than their customers.

I do not doubt that some people do not require competition to perform well (there are many public servants in this situation). It cannot be emphasized enough that law and order, state functions *par excellence*, should be financed by taxes and cannot be served by the market.

However, I know from experience that running these organizations without the stimulus of competition can be a challenge. Many scandals are currently coming to light.

Objectively speaking, most strikes in France occur in the public sector. It is easy to explain why: there is no competition, so it is easy to take users hostage. Being irreplaceable is an excellent way of putting pressure on management. Look at Marseille's dockers. This is definitely not the case of companies in competitive markets.

At the end of the day, what is the best solution? Organizations defending individual interests but regulated by competition and operating on a global scale, or organizations given monopolies over services because they supposedly serve the public interest?

Given current upheavals and the disastrous state of national finances, I think it is time to seriously ask ourselves the question.

Public interest, competition between states and reengineering the public sector

With globalization, the idea of inter-state competition is gaining ground.

Clearly, public sector efficiency varies from country to country. Traveling is one way this is visible. This efficiency is also visible in a country's growth rates, tax rates and finances. It is fascinating to compare a small country like Singapore – with $400 billion in cash for 4 million inhabitants and one of the lowest tax rates worldwide – with France, which has one of the world's highest tax rates, a debt of 1,500 billion euros ($2,111 billion) and 15 times the population.

The difference is amazing. By Singapore standards, France should have 6,000 billion euros ($8,447 billion) in cash instead of 1,500 billion euros ($2,111 billion) in debt. The difference is $150,000 per person, or three times France's annual GDP per capita. This cannot be caused by business, because the same companies are present in France and Singapore. The situation calls for a comparative analysis by the public sector and politicians.

International comparisons, and the competition this implies, now concern the public sector. It is no longer untouchable, as we used to believe. The public sector and business are both in the same boat.

The public sector can stimulate or dampen economic activity through industrial policies, for example. While these policies may have positive results, they are also financed by taxes – meaning they are just a transfer of resources. The investments are either financed by taxes that deprive other economic sectors of resources, or loans that our children must reimburse.[3]

The legal system, commercial law, employment law and competition law also contribute to creating an efficient or inefficient environment for companies.

Foreign trade is another important subject. France's balance of trade is in deficit. The government explains this by saying French SMEs export less than their German counterparts, or the country lacks companies employing over 250 persons. However, when you look more closely, it becomes clear that the German public sector is much less expensive than France's (around 9% of GDP). The German government is also implementing much bolder strategies to reduce public spending. Only by bringing its costs in line with Germany's and becoming competitive again will France improve its balance of trade and really defend society's interests.

Politicians must ensure the public sector remains competitive while respecting national differences. One after another, countries are reviewing their organizational structures and spending. This reengineering is having an impact. Canada, Sweden and New Zealand, for example, have completely changed the structure of their economic growth and public finances – it is an undeniable fact. I will come back to these examples in the next chapter.

After thinking long and hard about Mr. Juppé's comment, I came to the conclusion that defending the public interest could be as simple as thoroughly examining our public sector, to determine whether or not it is well adapted to the future.

---

3. See Bastiat's text "Harmful Remedies" (Appendices).

FIVE CASE STUDIES

Staying competitive is a challenge companies face daily. As a result, they are constantly adapting. The threat of going under keeps them on their toes. In the private sector, adaptation is second nature.

It takes much longer to detect when the public sector is uncompetitive. This is because, since George Pompidou's death, debt has allowed France to put its problems off until tomorrow. Before then, Charles de Gaulle and Georges Pompidou practically eliminated France's debt and balanced the budget.

The Greek financial crisis is a welcome wake-up call. Up until now, no one thought countries could be insolvent. Now we know it is possible. Most people agree that the public sector needs reform. Those who claim the market economy is to blame and think companies should pay more taxes are increasingly few. We are gradually coming to the conclusion that, without public sector reform, our whole society is doomed.

We are also realizing that profitable companies require an efficient and competitive public sector. Globalization concerns all sectors of the economy.

Budget deficits (whether run up by the left or the right) have always infuriated me as an individual. The fact that they are minimized by comparing them to GDP instead of tax revenue does not help. Today, we are running at an operating deficit of around 20%.

In my opinion, deficits signal errors. They indicate we have overspent on a given good or service. Temporary deficits can help solve the problem. But not a deficit that lasts 30 years! Our politicians, no matter their position on the political spectrum, should at least take responsibility for this situation. Why put the blame on companies?

I dislike debt, unless it is strategic debt like at Beneteau in 1976 or Essilor in 2000. This kind of debt helps further strategies. When things improve, it is immediately paid off.

I have never liked the expression "state money" because it implies there are no limits. We are the ones giving money to the state through our taxes. State money is our money!

Even in global businesses, I know how difficult it is to pay salaries in France and make money in competitive environments. I dare to hope that this is common knowledge.

I also pay taxes willingly when the money is used well.

French politicians and public servants must deal with this problem, identified by Michel Pébereau, chairman of the French bank BNP, in his report *Des finances publiques au service de notre avenir* (State Finances Building our Future). If they do not, the IMF will. The consequences are not pretty, as I witnessed in Argentina.

I hope politicians realize that France's GDP per capita ranking began falling in 1974, when the country started borrowing (France has dropped almost one place per year for the last 30 years). Many things indicate that state intervention outside the area of law and order and the resulting debt have slowed the nation's growth.

The text that follows is based on my observations of other countries as a French citizen. I have seen many things in my 40 years spent traveling the planet (my average was 315,000 miles a year!). This includes the British recovery under Margaret Thatcher, the US recovery under Ronald Reagan, the fall of Carlos Menem in Argentina, the rise of Canada under Jean Chrétien, the rise of New Zealand under Roger Douglas and the extraordinary growth of Singapore under Lee Kuan Yew.

As someone who is attached to his country, I would also like to give some suggestions based on the transformations I have seen around the world. Because these events have had positive results, because citizens in these countries are proud of them, and because they can now calmly turn their attention to the future.

When people talk about the advantages of globalization, the French always underline their own unique qualities. "We're different!" they say. In every domain, it seems, there is a French exception. This behavior has always surprised me, because I have learned many valuable things from the extremely rich cultures I have encountered.

When Americans and Asians observe cultural differences, they ask themselves what this can teach them. Americans systematically see change as progress, not a threat. Asians are fundamentally curious. They do not see imitation as servility, but a form of respect. As time went by, I found myself doing the same. I discovered that comparative analysis was an excellent way of getting to know yourself and boosting your creativity.

Let me be perfectly clear: I think the "French exception" is a form of arrogance. We must change quickly or suffer the consequences.

Seeking out better practices in our competitors is one of Essilor's strengths. As a regular individual – and not just a businessman – I have observed successful reforms in other countries, and I think France would be foolish not to take note.

Canada and public sector reform

In Canada, Essilor has an excellent subsidiary with one of the group's most steady growth rates. It was in Canada that we tested our laboratory purchase and integration strategy. We then implemented this strategy in the US and the rest of the world. Our Canadian subsidiary is one of our pioneers. Civil society is young, dynamic and mobile. The pioneer culture is strongly anchored in local traditions. We witnessed the reform launched in the early 1990s.

I have been talking about Canada's turnaround in France for the last 15 years. I must admit people are beginning to listen to me. Better late than never.

In 1993, Jean Chrétien launched a reform with remarkable scope. When they talk about public sector reform in Canada, this does not mean stabilizing spending as it does in France. It means decreasing federal spending by 18.9% in three years. In France, what we consider "cutting back" does not even come close.

The most important thing I learned from the Canadian reform was that the catastrophes predicted by some economists – a fall in economic growth and social unrest – never happened. Canada may have had luck on its side (a good economic outlook and a drop in the Canadian dollar). But today the country is in good shape and it came through the recent economic crisis relatively unscathed.

Canadians are proud of what their country has achieved, and have published many articles on the subject. Their message goes against the things we hear in France every day. Cutting back does not harm growth after all.

In 1993, Canada was in a similar situation as France is today. Public debt was around 100% of GDP and the budget deficit was around 9%.

The Canadians considered that if they did not take action, the country would lose its fiscal and economic sovereignty. They therefore decided to reduce the federal budget by nearly 20%, with two conditions. First, statutory deductions would not be cut until spending had drop by the desired amount (19%). Secondly, surplus funds would be put towards reducing debt, lowering taxes and developing ambitious projects for the future (in research, development and education). Major communication campaigns were launched to explain this reform to the general public. Government spending was reduced at the same time as public sector spending. Contributions were spread across all socio-professional categories. Trade unions were eventually convinced, and they were unable to muster up much opposition to a reform that was both needed and well balanced. After years of tax increases, Canadians were aware that there was a structural problem they needed to deal with. It made competition impossible, especially with the US.

This all dates back 15 years. Since then, spending has dropped. The figure of 19% is deceiving, because it hides the 50% spending cuts experienced in some ministries. Only the Ministry of Aboriginal Affairs has increased its budget.

The results are almost unbelievable: debt has been divided by three, there is now a budget surplus of 1% (instead of a deficit of 9%), and GDP has begun growing again. Of course, the exchange rate did dropped 25%. With hindsight, Canadian economists think that shifting spending from the public to the private sector "has probably had a positive effect on growth." The only "failure" is "the lack of control over regional spending." It seems to good to be true.

We lived through this period. There was no drama, the people were calm. They knew that someone – Jean Chrétien – had finally taken things into his own hands. Someone had to do it after all.

New Zealand under Roger Douglas: the most ambitious healthcare reform in the world

New Zealand's public finances in the 1990s

In the 1990s, New Zealand's healthcare system was run by the public sector and took up a big chunk of GDP. Without reforms, the books would never balance.

At that time, New Zealand's situation was very similar to France's today. Growth was slower than the OECD average, public debt was around $20,000 per household, the country was insolvent and there had been a budget deficit for the last 40 years.

New Zealand owes its turnaround to Roger Douglas. Douglas is an interesting man: he is the son of a farmer and had a difficult childhood. He worked in manufacturing before taking up politics later in life as a member of the Labour Party. He was named Minister of Finance before being elected Prime Minister. He is extremely intelligent: he takes philosophical concepts and transforms them into real policies. This is what sets him apart.

He completely rebuilt the New Zealand economy by changing the balance between the public and private sectors (through taxes, the labor market, budget cuts, reimbursing national debt, balancing the budget and overhauling the education, retirement and health systems).

New Zealanders talk passionately about this period, during which the country took off. The high point came when New Zealand won the America's Cup.

Douglas laid down two very simple principles: individual responsibility, and trust in competitive systems. His reform targeted the most disadvantaged populations. He wanted people of all walks of life to make decisions and assume responsibility for the things that concerned them. His reasoning is so clear it can be quoted:

"We need a tax benefit system which guarantees a decent standard of living without sending out the wrong signals which discourage work and encourage dependency."

"The aim is to put the underprivileged in the same position as anyone else as far as possible"

"Any form of assistance must leave them with their dignity intact. It should still allow them to make the sorts of choices available to those around them."

"In simple terms, we have to give people a reason to work."

"One of the most serious problems in free or paying welfare systems like France's, for example, is that they prevent people from making their own decisions. Making decisions is what builds personalities, it helps us learn from our mistakes and trust in our successes. Giving people the right to choose respects their dignity and encourages personal development."

"Basically, even if we help people, they have to be in a position to make their own decisions."

If plans for healthcare reform in France always fail, it is because there is are underlying issues that must be resolved. It is much more than just a question of good or bad management.

New Zealand's biggest reform was in the healthcare sector. Because so many public resources were taken up by healthcare, balancing the budget (and kick-starting growth) necessarily meant overhauling the health system. The New Zealand experience deserves our attention. Free healthcare was considered a right, as it is in France. Thanks to Douglas, free healthcare was no longer seen as a right, but an opportunity.

"Most New Zealanders have come to believe that a wide range of health services will be available, as of right, when they want them. In reality the system falls well short of this..."

"But government cannot do everything for everyone. All the technological possibilities of modern medicine cannot be made available... nor can people avoid responsibility for their own health in the expectation that outside agencies will protect them or repair the effects of their neglect..."

"Since 1938 no political party in power has fundamentally changed the structure of medical care delivery, and the poor have been major losers."

"Users are unable to minimize inefficiencies or look for the most efficient solutions by themselves. Doctors are not rewarded when they find ways of satisfying demand. The reason for this failure is that normal market processes have been replaced by laws, regulations and bureaucracy."

In theory

The system is based on the idea that individuals take out insurance for "serious problems, that are relatively unlikely but that cost a lot of money, like hospitalization, because they must pay market prices."

In return, they get... a tax cut.

The government helps out those who cannot afford insurance (by giving them vouchers), but "individuals are free to choose their own insurance company, the choice is not made for them."

The old healthcare system was split into five competing insurance companies.

Parliament decides which treatments are insured.

Health insurance contracts last one year. Insurers cannot cancel policies or refuse renewals. There is no national database.

The terms of reimbursement must encourage individuals to take care of their health and do their best to prevent illness (through bonuses, like for car insurance).

Insurance prices are set by the market, and insurers can define different categories of individuals based on risk. Insurers can establish lists of approved doctors and hospitals.

Top-level research and experimentation is still governed by the public sector.

In practice

Competition between insurers has made the healthcare system much more efficient upstream.

The hospital system has been restructured by treatment offered and geographical area.

Costs have dropped considerably. By making insurers compete with one another, the health system has become partly privatized, as doctors and their staff bought hospitals from the state.

They became entrepreneurs!

New techniques and practices have been introduced (home birth, for example, has been modernized and is increasingly popular).

The most unexpected effects of the reform appeared in prevention: smoking and drinking have decreased.

This all started 20 years ago. The reform lasted ten years. One thing is sure: New Zealand has found a lasting solution to its healthcare problems, because this system is based on solid principles. If New Zealand had not overhauled its healthcare system, which cost the government too much money, economic growth would have been impossible. It is certainly food for thought.

"Don't tell anyone Mr. Fontanet, but I need the private sector to manage the public sector." (Jean-Pierre Chevènement)

The model has made it to France, to a small region formerly shunned by central government. This example shows how a little competition goes a long way.

The text that follows pays homage to the secondary school teachers of Vendée, whether in private or public schools. They could represent a source of progress for our secondary schools, whose importance is growing as competition between international education systems increases.

I lived five years in the Vendée region when my wife and I worked at Beneteau under Annette Roux. We lived in Saint-Gilles-Croix-de-Vie, a small town split between farmland and the sea, which saw a lot of activity in the summer. I must admit that when we decided to move there, the Parisians in us, who went to the right schools in the right neighborhoods, worried about our three daughters: would they pay for their parents' career choices?

Our daughters were happy at school, and had good teachers, whether at Saint Gille's public or private schools. This experience did not hold them back at all. On the contrary, they enjoyed their time there, and were taught by some excellent teachers. Later on in life, they enrolled in some of France's finest schools, and this is no doubt due in part to their time in Vendée.

Initially, we enrolled two of our daughters at a public school and one at a private school. The girls quickly fit in, and we got along well with their teachers, who were all very interesting. In small towns, teachers have a unique status. We were invited to some teachers' homes. Others were members of the local council or tennis club. We got to know them well, which helped us smooth over any problems our children had at school.

The thing that surprised us most of all was the visits we got from school principals trying to persuade us to send our daughters to their school. These visits always led to interesting debates during which we were able to give our opinion on the education our children received.

We quickly realized that these extremely courteous visits were the result of fierce competition between local schools. Each principal wanted the best students for his or her school, and the Fontanet girls were part of this battle.

Teachers' motivation was directly linked to their local market share. This is somewhat of a taboo in France, but the Vendée example shows how competition in the education system is not destructive at all. It can even be stimulating.

A few years later, Jean-Pierre Chevènement, who was Minister of Education at the time, invited me to meet with him. When he asked me about my girls' education, I told him this story with gusto.

He then said something that I can now quote, given it was some 20 years ago: "Mr. Fontanet, don't tell anyone, but I need the private sector to manage the public sector."

In this changing world, and in a field as complex as education, organizations cannot operate correctly by themselves. New methods, comparison and competition are the best ways of finding solutions.

Lee Kuan Yew's vision for the future

Singapore is, without a doubt, the country I have visited with the most impressive and enduring growth rate. After starting out with nothing in 1963, Singaporeans today hold the world record in GDP per capita. They live on a mountain of cash (as mentioned in the previous chapter), despite having no natural resources and one of the lowest tax rates in the world. I have never lived in Singapore, but I have visited many times. Each time, I was impressed by the progress being made.

Lee Kuan Yew was Singapore's prime minister, but also its founding father and strategist for 47 years.

Every year, he held dinners for businessmen who have invested in Singapore. This is how I got the opportunity to speak with him several times. The dinner was always very informal. Everyone could ask questions. He had an answer for everything. Talking to him was like experiencing history in the making. He was the only living leader who knew Winston Churchill, Charles de Gaulle, Richard Nixon and Mao Zedong. His achievements beat those of all the other world leaders hands down. What he said was sometimes harsh, but always very clear. That's what I heard and understood.

"Whatever your job is, it's better than being on welfare."

"Change hurts, but… it's better to suffer now than experience the shame in decline."

"To swim with the big fish, you have to ensure your people's talents are up there on the international level."

"My duty is to give you, international companies, the best possible working conditions. Your duty is to make the most of them."

"Today, a country is not judged on its size, but on the skills of its population and the quality of its organization."

"Manufacturing policy in the traditional sense doesn't work in a country like Singapore, because international companies have become too strong. To benefit from globalization, you have to take advantage of their energy by making yourself the best host country."

Singapore's economic strategy, public sector management, tax system and administration are described in many books, which are accessible to all readers.[1]

Many of our problems could be solved by taking a leaf out of Singapore's book.

Egis and the Caisse des Dépôts

It is not true that economic liberals are against a strong public sector. This is a groundless accusation. We are in favor of the public sector concentrating its efforts on law and order. Many think, myself included, that more investment is needed to help it come to terms with new challenges, especially in the fields of justice, defence and the police force.

---

1. See Bibliography.

However, given current levels of national debt, the public sector must withdraw from activities that could safely be run by competitive markets.

The Egis example is an excellent case in point.

Egis is an engineering company and a subsidiary of Caisse des Dépôts, a French financial organization. The origins, history, and performance of this discreet company make it worth a closer look.

Over the years Egis, which could be described as a spinoff of the French administration hosted by the *Caisse des Dépôts* has brought together different public sector entities, including the government's operational branch, the *Ministère de l'Équipement* (Ministry of Infrastructure). It is a widely known fact that France's excellent infrastructures (road, railway and communications networks) give the country a comparative advantage. This is the result of our unique intelligence, a combination of logic and flexibility.

This policy originated with the *Corps des Ponts et Chaussées* (Bridge and Highway Corps), founded by Napoleon, whose engineers (including Gustave Eiffel) invented many technological innovations (such as reinforced concrete, prestressed concrete and bridge design). It should therefore come as no surprise that French civil engineering companies (such as Bouygues, Vinci and Eiffage) are some of the best in the world in their field.

Egis quickly began competing with private engineering companies in strategic markets in France and abroad: road, rail, water, urban development and aeronautics. Thanks to an ambitious internal development plan and market concentration, it is today one of Europe's leading engineering companies. The sector is still being consolidated so companies are able to compete on the global market, as seen in Egis' alliance with Iosis in 2010. At this time, Egis followed Iosis' example and gave 400 top executives a significant stake in the company (plus a block of shares set aside for employees via a company investment fund). Employees now own 25% of the company's capital, the balance being held by the Caisse des Dépôts.

Today, Egis is making a breakthrough on international markets. Its expansion in India is nothing short of remarkable. Egis could become a world leader. The figures say it all: in 2010, sales reached 800 million euros ($1,125 million), and the group employed 10,000 people. Egis is profitable, has very little debt and its turnover has grown over 10% per year for the last few years. Egis operates in over 100 countries worldwide.

The example of Egis and the Caisse des Dépôts is extremely relevant given today's public sector restructuring. Infrastructural engineering is an area where authorities can choose to build public infrastructures themselves or oversee this work by awarding contracts based on pre-defined specifications to private companies competing against each other.

Basically, this "outsourcing" is a way of sharing expertise between countries in areas of state intervention that do not come under the banner of law and order. It is also a way of taking advantage of competition and global economies of scale. What is more, by putting these activities under market control, the public sector could also make money from the experience it has gained. The money earned could be put towards paying off its debt.

Giving employees a stake in these companies is probably the best way of compensating them for losing their "civil servant" status. Employee shareholding is also an excellent way of encouraging teams to do all they can to make this new experience a positive one and sharing the value created.

Good luck to the Caisse des Dépôts, good luck to Egis!

PART VI

FRANCE VS. THE REST OF THE WORLD

FRANCE'S FEARS
VS. THE FRENCH TOUCH

I am very suspicious of what people call the "French exception".

Under Charles de Gaulle, this term was used to defend national interests and French *grandeur*. Today, however, whenever discussion turns to a successful economic strategy implemented abroad, the immediate reaction is, "Oh, that wouldn't work here." The French exception has all too often become a form of arrogance that leads to conservatism.

There are historical reasons for this. I hope that the overview that follows will show why the country is resistant to the market economy and business.

The Age of Enlightenment had an important impact on French society. So too did two historical figures: Jean-Baptiste Colbert, who served under Louis XIV, and the omnipresent Jean-Jacques Rousseau.

During the Enlightenment, France was the intellectual center of the world. We are proud of this heritage, although we sometimes tend to believe the world still revolves around us. In reality, the English and the Dutch caught up to us back in the 18th century, because they understood the market economy faster than we did. Paradoxically the Age of Enlightenment worked better for them than for us!

The legacy of Colbert and Rousseau still weighs heavily on us. The time has come to talk about it and measure its impact. It has become a kind of obsession with us. Obsessions are always easier to deal with once we become aware of them.

Jean-Baptiste Colbert

Jean de la Fontaine did us no favors with his 17th century fable *The Milkmaid and the Milk Jug*. It is true that Perette, who spills her milk while dreaming of the money she will make, is a little negligent. However, even though she lacks in realism, she is still a budding entrepreneur. I am not sure it was a good thing to mock her and then teach this fable to 400 million French children. This is no laughing matter: Perette probably has something to do with the French people's suspicion for business. Without giving the fable more importance than it is due, it does raise the question: was doing business already looked down on under Louis XIV and Colbert?

At the time, economics was gaining ground throughout Europe, especially in France, Great Britain, the Netherlands and Scandinavia. The influence of Venice and Spain was waning, and French industry was just getting off the ground.

The French exception was Louis XIV's court. When someone made a bit of money through trade, they sold their business and bought land. They then came to the court to request a *concession d'État*, seen as a safe investment. These investments were the precursor of the public sector, already so present in the French mindset. At the time, the king only took 10% of national wealth. But Colbert had to make concessions to balance the budget, which was in deficit as a result of the king's endless wars. These deals were in hot demand. This no doubt contributed to the erroneous ideas that profitable companies were those that made the most of public handouts, and that profits were the result of political backscratching.

Meanwhile, rich Dutch and British businessmen continued to invest in companies. For them, real nobility was in trade. Their money was not spent on clothes, carriages or festivities, but on businesses into which they pumped all their savings. This was the beginning of the cultural divide between them and us. Our opulent parties no longer tempted them. The revocation of the Edict of Nantes and the resulting loss of brains and capital did the rest.[1]

---

1. Translator's note: issued by Henry IV in 1598, the Edict of Nantes gave religious freedom to his Protestant subjects, the Huguenots. By revoking it in 1685, Louis XIV forced these groups into exile.

During Louis XIV's reign, France was as rich as Great Britain, Germany, the Netherlands and the Americas. Now, 250 years later, France only accounts for 8% of economic activity in these countries. Its annual growth rate lags around 1% behind. This seems like a small difference, but when long-term growth varies between 2 and 3% per year (according to Immanuel Wallerstein), this amounts to 40%. In the long term, one small percentage point makes a big difference.

At the time, Louis XIV represented the state, and the state inspired – or was supposed to inspire – the whole nation. Colbert was his right-hand man. Society was mixed up with the state. Things cannot have been quite this simple, because Colbert was infuriated by his envoys' reports that, in the Netherlands, a republic, things ran smoothly.

These reports stated that everyone worked a lot to earn a salary or make a profit, that "invisible but active force." They also explained that the rich did not show off their riches, unlike in France. This was because they risked all their money by reinvesting in business, with the full knowledge of their employees. They told him that society was harmonious. Everyone lived in the same areas. The nation's elite did not live apart from the people, like at Versailles (a disastrous decision if ever there was one).

Even worse, when Colbert sought to compete with Dutch companies on neutral ground outside Europe, he failed miserably. Our children should be taught more about the victories of the privately funded Dutch East India Company over France's state-owned companies, mere shadows of their Dutch counterparts. Colbert's companies were only successful when they had monopolies in France. They were much less brilliant up against competitors.

Colbert was, however, an expert when it came to collecting taxes in regions under state control. "The art of taxation consists in fleecing people so they give maximum fleece with minimum struggle." In this field, he beat the Dutch hands down.

This "ancient history" has left its mark on France. Many brilliant entrepreneurs chose to leave the country at a key moment in the country's history. In my 40 years spent traveling around the world, I have met many people whose families left France during this time. The brain drain is a taboo subject, and its effects are difficult to quantify. However, many people seem to have left France in the last ten years. It would be interesting to know what impact this has on growth. In my humble opinion, a report on this subject is required.

Jean-Jacques Rousseau

Our other omnipresent ancestor is Jean-Jacques Rousseau. In French schools, one of his most widely read texts is the *Discourse on the Origin and Foundations of Inequality Among Men.*

"As long as men were content with the rustic huts, as long as they were limited to making their clothing out of skins sewn together with thorns or fish bones, adorning themselves with feathers and shells, painting their bodies with various colors, perfecting or embellishing their bows and arrows, using sharp-edged stones to make some fishing canoes or some crude musical instruments; in a word, as long as they applied themselves exclusively to tasks that a single individual could do and to the arts that did not require the cooperation of several hands, they lived as free, healthy, good and happy as they could in accordance with their nature; and they continued to enjoy among themselves the sweet reward of independent intercourse. But as soon as one man needed the help of another, as soon as one man realized that it was useful for a single individual to have provisions for two, equality disappeared, property came into existence, labor became necessary. Vast forests were transformed into smiling fields which had to be watered with men's sweat, and in which slavery and misery were soon seen to germinate and grow with the crops."

With such splendid prose, how can you resist such sentences? There is no more radical rejection of trade and the market economy. The economy spells the end of equality! It is but slavery and misery! But was the old world as good as all that? That's the million-dollar question. Let us move on:

"The first person who, having enclosed a plot of ground, took it into his head to say *this is mine* and found people simple enough to believe him, was the true founder of civil society. What crimes, wars, murders, what miseries and horrors would the human race have been spared had someone pulled up the stakes or filled in the ditch and cried out to his fellow-men: 'Do not listen to this imposter. You are lost if you forget that the fruits of the earth belong to all and the earth to no one!'"

The earth belongs to no one: ownership provokes war and destruction!

Jean-Jacques Rousseau is one of France's most prestigious historical figures. He also developed a strict form of socialism – dare we say
communism – with a little ecology thrown in.

It is quite clear that, in rejecting labor and ownership, Rousseau
is not very well inclined towards the market economy. Labor is not
considered in a favorable light – it is as if it could be taken back, or
the things we earned did not belong to us. It is something suspicious.
Ownership is a source of "misery and horrors." This does not bode
well for companies, private initiative or added value.

Why do French children not learn more about Voltaire, whose
hobby was gardening?

Under Rousseau's system, wealth belongs to everyone. The state
collects this wealth through taxes and redistributes it, but without analyzing the effect this has on creation. This logic can have tragi-comic
results, as seen in Trotsky's comment to the effect that "forced labor is
justified by the loss of motivation caused by the abolition of profits."
When people no longer profit from their labor or personal initiative,
the cudgel becomes the only practical solution.

Colbert and Rousseau unwittingly worked together year after year
to strengthen the state. Despite this, French companies have come a
long way in the last 20 years.

The French exception is that both the right wing – long influenced
by Colbert – and the left wing work together to increase state influence. The first considers the state is best placed to drive society, and
the second sees the state as the only entity capable of redistributing
wealth. Both agree high tax rates are necessary – either to invest on
society's behalf or to redistribute more wealth. Both are suspicious of
the private sector – one because it doubts its energy, and the other
because it does not trust the private sector to redistribute wealth fairly.
Between the two are French businesses and the private sector, fighting
(and deserving) to move forward.

Colbert and Rousseau have always had critics. These intellectuals and entrepreneurs earned much less praise, but were active and
efficient. They also built France, discretely and with considerable
effort – not to mention ingenuity, at times. Their names are Voltaire,
the Marquis of Vauban, the Marquis of Louvois, Benjamin Constant,
Alexis de Tocqueville, Frédéric Bastiat, Ferdinand de Lesseps and
Gustave Eiffel. More recent examples include Guy Sorman, Alain

Peyrefitte, Jean-Claude Casanova, Michel Albert, Marcel Dassault, Francis Bouygues, Antoine Riboud, François Dalle, Olivier Lecerf, Claude Bébear and Gérard Mulliez, among others.

Despite these cultural barriers and a negative image abroad, an increasing number of international studies have shown that French business and businessmen have made a major breakthrough in the last 20 years. French companies listed in Europe have had the best results. Serge Blanchard demonstrates this brilliantly in his recent book, *Notre Avenir Dépend d'Eux* (Our Future Depends on Them). Who knew that the 250 largest listed companies created more wealth over the last 40 years than the state has created in debt? Not to mention the fact that the debt contracted by the state actually slowed them down!

If the French state worked with business, and not against it, France would still be one of the world's top ranking companies in terms of GDP per capita.

Today's businesses and businessmen are the torchbearers for their illustrious ancestors and freedom fighters.

WHAT'S SO GREAT
ABOUT THE JAPANESE?

Every year, I present our strategy to Essilor's works council. It is an enjoyable event where we have intense and valuable discussions with employee representatives. In theory, discussion is limited to the French mother company. In practice, we talk about Essilor worldwide. I generally give the same speech I gave to analysts, so everyone has the same information.

On this particular occasion, I had just gotten back from Japan. I was a little jetlagged, but extremely happy with the way things were progressing with our joint venture with Nikon.

Our decision to attack Hoya on their home turf was an extremely risky one. It was also an excellent opportunity to work with Nikon, an emblematic company in Japan.

Nikon's teams worked unbelievably hard. Initially, we had made some very difficult decisions, such as freezing salaries for three years and relocating some production to Thailand. We had come to an agreement with trade unions: they knew we were starting from scratch and Hoya would be looking to attack early on.

We immediately trusted each other. Our market share held steady after the first attack and slowly began increasing. Customers liked the joint venture idea. Things were coming together. It is an amazing feeling when you know your plan is working. Dialogue with our Japanese counterparts improved daily. Their trust in us increased as they realized what we could bring them, especially in terms of production. Meanwhile, we were gaining valuable knowledge of the Japanese market, which had been completely unfathomable to us prior to the joint venture.

Joint ventures depend on both parties getting to know each other. This can take some time. However during my most recent trip to Japan, something remarkable had happened. We had suddenly broken down the barriers and started confiding in each other. Each side understood and appreciated the other. We were happy to be on the same team, and we were winning our first major battles (big contracts with customers). Our new products were taking off, the team was working well together and I felt people were happy to be at work. It was exhausting but exhilarating. I had really come to admire the Japanese: their bravery in business, their sense of service, their ability to do things well, their precision, their attention to detail and, perhaps above all, their technical prowess in unexpected technological fields.

They appreciated our creativity, our positive attitude, our ability to sum things up, our resourcefulness, and our somewhat disobedient mentality. Our use of abstract concepts fascinated them. We write differently, because our grammar is based on a different form of logic. They use ideograms. To make sense of these characters, you have to have an excellent memory and attention to detail. Our brains were programmed differently, and it was interesting to see these differences at work on a daily basis.

One day, to lighten the atmosphere after a long day at the office, I compared the budget we were working on to the battle of Austerlitz. I think they were astounded. The next day, they told me how much they enjoyed this unexpected comparison, which was edifying but a real cultural shock. They also pointed out that I had mixed up the roles played by Soult and Murat. They had spent the night poring over encyclopedias!

So when I arrived in France, I was tired but happy.

As usual, I began my speech to the central works council with a quick summary of Essilor "around the world." When I had finished, one of the employee representatives said, "Mr. Fontanet, when you talk about Japan and the US, you seem happy, but when you talk about France, you look sad. Do we need to speak Japanese or English to interest you? What's so great about them?"

What a fantastic question! The meeting had gotten off to a great start; we were definitely going to have fun. I immediately forgot my fatigue.

However, my head was spinning. Of course I love my country. It gave me everything I have: loving parents, a happy family and good schools. I have only met extraordinary people in the companies I have worked for (BCG, Beneteau, Eurest and Essilor). I owe them a lot: Bruce, John, François, Louis Claude, Annette, Gérard, Philippe, Jacques, Henri, Philippe, Olivier, Patrick, Claude and all the others who helped me become the person I am today.

France also means the regions I love: Brittany and Savoy. I remember the doctors that cared for my daughters after they had serious accidents. I also remember the brilliant teachers that changed my life.

However, France also means the 35-hour working week, endlessly exercising our "rights," the endless strikes, the public debt that saddens me deeply, and our drop in the international rankings. I think of all my American, Chinese, Indian, Japanese and Korean friends: Chuck, Rick, He Yi, Jayanth, CT Lee, Enya, Yoshida, Kariya, Kimura and the others I cannot name for lack of space. I work with them, and we are very close, much closer than I am to many of my fellow countrymen. We have the same vision of the world, work, duty and people.

This makes me think of a recent trip I took to India. We were completing due diligence before signing a joint venture agreement with a family business whose laboratory was based in a slum. Half the employees in the companies we buy live in slums. They have an incredibly difficult life, but still manage to be happy. They consider their slum is a society. They know the turnover for each small factory. They know the countries they export to. They are proud to see sales figures increase year after year. After experiencing something like this, it is difficult to sympathize with strikes in France. It is impossible for me to understand strikes when they drag on so long that Essilor employees are exhausted by coming to work. Some of them get up at 4 am to get to work on time. That dedication is the real France for me. I am always afraid there will be strikes when our major clients visit. They travel a long way and our meetings are sometimes planned six months in advance. We organize an extraordinary program and then it all goes down the drain. The last time there was a strike, our customers missed their return flight. A whole day lost! What must these countries think of us?

This does not mean people should not be able to strike. Strikes are a legitimate way of showing there is a problem with dialogue in the company. But strikes are misused in France. Thanks to a few unscrupulous people, strikes have become a source of exasperation for the French people. This is unacceptable. To tell the truth, I sometimes feel more Indian or Chinese than French.

Anyway, back to the works council. I said to the audience, "To answer your question, let me tell you a few anecdotes."

I told them about when we closed Park Street, our biggest American plant (at the time, it had 1,200 employees). It had stopped being competitive in the 2000s because it used techniques that had been adopted in Asia. Closure was our only option.

"We did things properly by telling the employees early on, paying for retraining and helping them find new jobs. The American market is so flexible, they easily found work. Back in 2007, most people found a new job within two months. The plant was in Florida, so most people switched professions – they found work in accommodation, catering, tourism or construction, without too many problems. In France, the trade unions would have talked about "downgrading" or "odd jobs." They have a completely different way of looking at things. On the last day, the employees at this plant sent me the last lens they had made, along with this message: 'Mr. Fontanet, we stood strong until the end. We're proud of our achievements. Here is the last of the 500 million lenses we produced at this plant over the last 30 years. We would like to thank you for everything Essilor did for us over this period.' "

I kept speaking.

"France isn't America. French newspapers sometimes present Americans badly, by saying they're too materialistic. For me, America is the letter I got from Essilor's employees."

You could have heard a pin drop.

I went on. "Americans understand that consumer freedom depends on producer freedom. Why doesn't change scare them? Because they trust the system, and because they believe that each change means a new opportunity."

"In France, when things change, we ask ourselves, 'What do I stand to lose?' In the US, they ask, 'What do I stand to gain?' "

"Americans understand that, in a world where consumers are free to buy what they choose, there is no such thing as permanent employee advantages. You're lucky you work for a good company with an increasing market share. But let's be perfectly clear. Things work so well at Essilor because everyone works hard, from the most unskilled employees to the CEO. If we started losing market share, some advantages would have to go."

"The US public sector is completely different from ours. The state isn't there to say 'I'll protect you.' The state says, 'Take care of yourself, our society is open. I promise that if you work hard, you'll go far. Of course, not everyone is equal, but I promise that you will make progress.' "

"The Americans believe that tomorrow will be a better day. For them, safety means flexibility. They believe in the market economy. Their attitude to success is completely different to ours. Americans aren't jealous of other people's success. They say, 'If they succeed, so can I.' In my opinion, we need to take a leaf out of their book. Being jealous is ridiculous. Wanting to see someone successful fail is like shooting yourself in the foot: you only hurt yourself. Americans understand this."

Someone in the audience asked, "What about the Japanese and the Koreans?"

"They're very different. They Japanese and Koreans are taught from an early age that they live in small countries surrounded by giants. They learn that they don't have natural resources and that the big crush the small. They're taught that they must work harder than everyone else and present a united front. Examples of little people like Tintin and Asterix triumphing over giants work for us but aren't believable for the Japanese. Over there, big countries always dominate the small ones. So the moral of the story is that everyone must work together and stand strong. The Japanese always put the group first. Individual interests are always less important than those of the group. In Japan, the state doesn't play an important role; companies rule. Politicians are much less prestigious than company directors, so the idea of a protective state doesn't exist. The welfare state has no meaning for the Japanese. Companies are everything. When things go badly, employees are ready to do anything to help their company get back on its feet. [I remind them how we froze salaries for three years at Nikon.] Do you think we could have done that here? Of course, after the three years were up, Nikon Essilor was extremely generous. Employees were given four months salary as a bonus. But when we initially asked them to make sacrifices, they agreed. And I can tell you they worked very hard."

"These are the people France must compete with. So just remember one thing: whatever your culture, whether you're French, American or Japanese, you still need to work hard. If you don't, you'll end up paying for it one day. This is the only way to keep things positive. Work hard and think of Essilor!"

"Now, to come back to your initial question, are they better workers than you?"

"The answer is absolutely not. You work just as well as our Japanese and American employees."

"There is no reason to worry, you're just as good as they are. The French work extremely well. French workers like to know where they're going. If they feel like they're not being told something, or they don't know the whole truth, things start deteriorating. You know, Napoleon, who knew many different cultures, said that French soldiers were different from others. They like being given a bit of freedom; they like knowing the battle plan in advance so they can fight well. When they understand, they are the best soldiers in the world, because they are very resourceful. But, if they're treated badly, things go downhill quickly."

"We're all a bit like that. We all have our qualities and our shortcomings."

"But it is Essilor and our customers who put food on our tables – no one else. Don't forget it. We have to go the extra mile for them. Our good working environment is thanks to their trust in us."

MR. AND MRS. MAZZONE

Jean-Pierre Mazzone is one of Essilor's employees who dedicated his life to helping us open plants around the world. When I returned from India in 2002, I had the honor of awarding him the *Légion d'honneur*, a French decoration he had earned for his contribution to business.

I think the speech I gave on this occasion gives a good idea of the qualities our expatriate employees all possess. They are, in some ways, a model for the French people.

X. Fontanet's speech to J.P. Mazzone
when awarding him the *Légion d'honneur*.
11 December 2002

Dear Jean-Pierre,

I cannot express how happy I was when I learned you were being awarded the Légion d'honneur. *Nowadays this distinction is given to well known people, who are close to power and graduates of the West's prestigious schools. Usually people pay no attention to those like you and Mireille (I would also like to pay tribute to your wife, Mireille) who have been doing the ground-work, far from the French capital, for long periods of time.*

This decoration, like those of Claude Brignon and Michel Terlon[1] is special. It's special because it comes from the French president's personal reserve, a reserve he wished to set aside for people that go unnoticed, because they are too far from the limelight or do not move in privileged circles. Essilor told him about you and your achievements. This is the reason behind your nomination. You didn't ask for it, you didn't expect it. That is why you really deserve it!

You earned this honor far from France, and far from the limelight, while setting up plants on the ground in Asia, while waiting your turn in line at foreign ministries. These plants' contributions to Essilor's current stability and prosperity are priceless. This is confirmed every year. All those here know how hard you have worked and under what difficult conditions. You have been constantly on the move, and lived your life precariously.

Setting up a plant is no picnic. In general, you started from scratch, in countries neither you nor Essilor were familiar with, armed with a suitcase and a mission: to set up or start production at an Essilor plant.

★
★ ★

Bataan, Philippines. I don't know how many of you have been to Bataan, but most of you would think it was jungle or virgin forest.

Jean-Pierre arrived in Bataan one morning in 1987, with his wife Mireille and two children, Florent, 17 months, and Pierre, 4 years old.

Let me stray from my subject here, and pay homage to Mireille, Pierre and Florent, as well as all the families of Essilor's expatriates. The best way I can do this is by telling you about our conversation over lunch.

I started out by asking Mireille what it was like arriving in a house without electricity or running water.

"No problem," said Mireille. "There was Evian. Health was the one thing I never cut corners on. Nothing was too expensive when it came to our children's welfare."

I then said, "Evian is good, but you were all alone, in a tiny village of 2,000 inhabitants, a long way from anywhere, with people who didn't speak your language. How did you deal with the isolation?"

---

1. Former collegues of Mr. Mazzone who received this decoration.

"It was a fantastic opportunity for the children, you have no idea how welcoming people are in Bataan. The boys spent their days at the beach, playing with canoes they made with local children. Mr. Fontanet, what better childhood could they have had? They were seeing different countries, living with simple and welcoming people, making toys out of nothing, learning another language at a young age, learning about what is important. You know, I think my children are more resourceful today because of this experience."

"What did you do when Pierre and Florent were sick? At their age, they must have fallen ill sometimes."

"Of course! We had a few problem with amoeba, but you know, the Filipinos have very good treatments for amoeba, and we were very well cared for, probably better than if we had been in Paris. When we arrived, I knew that Bataan had just experienced one of the worst tropical storms in its history. The village was damaged and most of the houses had been destroyed. It was a great start for us newcomers!"

I asked her what it was like living through a cyclone.

"Well, it's good to experience nature's fury. We forget it in France, where everyone lives in cities. It helps you get your priorities straight, and the way the villagers pulled together after the cyclone was one of the most extraordinary things I've ever seen."

"Solitude, cyclones, amoeba… Does nothing ever scare you?"

"Definitely! I was a bit scared once. I was putting away the children's toys, when a snake slid out of a watering can! I moved away, and it left me alone. Luckily I was the one who found it; can you imagine if it had been one of the boys? Actually, Mr. Fontanet, the only thing that worried me was my children's education. So I started teaching them and, you know, children adapt very quickly to new situations, the adults are the complicated ones. I wanted to move from Bataan to Manila for their schooling. Pierre and Florent couldn't spend their whole lives on the beach. I moved to Manila, and that was quite hard for me. To move all the way around the world and then find myself separated from my husband, who I only saw on weekends when he was tired and worried – that was hard. But the children didn't suffer, we were there for them, and they did well in their studies.

"At least it was safer in Manila," I said.

"Not at all, Mr. Fontanet! We lived through the political coup. It was crazy, we didn't know which way things would go. We even started running out of food. But people were so kind; we shared the basics with our neighbors. At times like that, you really understand what solidarity means."

Dear Mireille, listening to you, I suddenly felt very small.

*

* *

Claude then offered Jean-Pierre Thailand. If you'll allow me to be a little debonair and shorten this account – you lived through a few more hurricanes and a few more political coups (12 major events in total) before returning to France while Jean-Pierre helped launch our joint venture with Sola in India. You were with your two children, Pierre and Florent, who are now beginning their own lives and adapting well to the French system, thanks to the fact you always spoke French with them at home. They manage very well for themselves: now they are grown up and responsible for their own destinies. Their culture and past experiences will serve them well in the global environment that awaits them. You have fulfilled your duty towards them.

Jean-Pierre returned from India in 2002.

*

* *

Dear Jean-Pierre, dear Mireille, what can I say about two such momentous lives spent helping others? If everyone were like you, there would be paradise on Earth. Dear friends, share your experiences with us, they do us good, they remind us of what is really important and what makes us grow. You must find France rather small. Tell us simply and clearly your truths, they do us good. Share with us your strength and serenity. Other challenges await you, I'm sure. As I said to Claude and Michel, you have nothing left to prove and a lot left to enjoy! Mireille, Jean-Pierre, this medal is to honor you. It makes us extremely happy.

Jean-Pierre, on behalf of the French president and the power he has given us, we hereby name you a knight of the Légion d'honneur.

CONCLUSION:
WHAT DOES THE FUTURE HOLD?

I am always amazed at the progress made by people I have met during my working life: company directors, colleagues, employees, suppliers, partners and clients.

When people are given responsibility, at work for example, they can do unbelievable things. Of course, we are not all born with the same advantages, and each person starts out differently. However, no matter where we start from, we all have the ability to move forward. In reality, this is what really counts.

To me, there is no difference between a young engineering trainee who becomes a division director or an internationally recognized specialist in a new technology, and a young factory worker who becomes a senior trade union representative and makes a mark on the company. I am happy for both of them. They have both fulfilled their duty to the company and to society.

Companies are the ideal place for personal contributions and development. People contribute because companies must look after their customers – this is their reason for being. The company must be better than its competitors (otherwise its product does not sell). In competitive systems, sales are proof that companies contribute to the wellbeing of their customers.

People grow because companies are places where they are given responsibility. They make judgments, learn from their mistakes, and gain confidence from their successes.

A company that builds long-term relationships with customers and suppliers is taking part in sustainable development and furthering the public interest. Lasting business relationships ensure common interests are respected and both parties work towards what could be called the greater good. The differences between the public and private sectors are no longer meaningful: competitive companies further the public interest.

It is true that globalization is a tough battle, fought between competitors from different histories and cultures. However, it is also a fabulous opportunity for those who dare, because it gives people a chance to develop and learn new things. International companies are best placed to ensure people benefit from globalization.

French people do not see French companies in a favorable light. This is a shame because French companies that have gone global have survived the crisis well. This is proof that they can excel in competitive international environments.

The French may be a little disobedient, but they also take the initiative. They may love discussion and debate, but they can also deal with abstract ideas. They may be headstrong, but they are also enthusiastic. French people's faults are also the source of their best qualities.

A trusting environment helps convert this potential into positive energy. In these conditions, people take risks. They know they will be rewarded for making the right choices and given the opportunity to recover from making the wrong ones. Trust is a company's biggest asset.

Trust is not just trusting yourself, it is also trusting the system. It depends on setting appropriate strategic targets. Employees know when management makes mistakes, putting the company on the line. Trust and good strategy go hand in hand.

To develop France's potential, we must teach students (and politicians!) about competitive economies. The French school system does not prepare children to work in companies. It does not give young French people the intellectual tools or the economic grounding they need to thrive in the global economy. It is time to rewrite the economic textbooks.

What does the future hold?

There is no doubt that the global economy will grow in the next 50 years, for one simple reason: China, India and Latin America. The number of consumers will double to two billion at least. This alone is sufficient to ensure 25 years growth at 5% – possibly the highest rate the world has experienced to date.

This growth is an extraordinary opportunity for the 50 million companies operating in different businesses worldwide. In developed countries, the economy is already divided into hundreds of thousands of different businesses. With the development of new technologies and ideas resulting from the confrontation with new "players" in China, India and Latin America, new businesses will continue to support the growth of millions of companies.

For these reasons, we cannot call this situation a "crisis." This term may even lead to analytical errors.

There will be strong contrasts. Developed economies will grow more slowly than others, and technological change (Internet, energy efficiency and medical progress) will affect many markets. Residents of developed countries will have to be very flexible. Emerging economies will experience much faster and probably more sustained growth.

Countries will not be able to expand geographically. This is a good thing because it means peace. The public sector must therefore rejoice in the fact that companies stimulate civil society.

Western nations, and France in particular, have run up too much debt over the last 40 years. This is partly because they have chosen to intervene in areas where the market would probably manage activities much more efficiently. Unlike companies, countries do not consider they compete with one another (citizens do not change countries every day). Consequently, their costs and management methods are not monitored like those of companies. In France's case, for example, there are too many levels of government (six in total, from city councils to European institutions), each of which has generated its own bureaucracy. Today, Western nations are aware that they have serious financial problems. They now need to overhaul their strategies and focus on what should be their key activities: law and order, and reducing sovereign debt.

In this book, I have suggested several ideas that have been successfully tested abroad (in Sweden and Canada, for example). In taking the bull by the horns, these countries have shown that considerable progress can be made in a short space of time. Obviously, the public sector has a supervisory role to play in financial markets, especially in areas where abuses have had a negative effect on companies.

France is a country that attracts considerable foreign investment. It is a beautiful country, which is a major advantage. However, it must reduce its excessive taxes and bureaucracy. If it supports its big firms (it must be really proud of them) and attracts foreign companies, it has nothing to fear from the future.

But it is impossible to go further and claim to know what the future holds. Only manipulators embark on this perilous exercise. No one knows what will really happen, and this uncertainty is central to systems built around freedom.

In these kinds of situations, real security comes from being confident, audacious and competitive, lowering operating costs and contracting reasonable levels of debt. In other words, trust yourself, your company and your country to allow you to remain flexible. Real security comes from being more mobile, more daring and less expensive than your competitors.

If this book helps people understand that trust is the best gamble for the future, it has not been in vain.

APPENDICES

SELECTIVE BIBLIOGRAPHY

BASTIAT, Frédéric, *The Bastiat Collection* (2nd ed.), Ludwig von Mises Institute, Auburn, Alabama, 2007.

BLANCHARD, Serge, *Notre avenir dépend d'eux*, François Bourin, Paris, 2010.

Boston Consulting Group (BCG), *Perspective on Experience*, Boston, MA, The Boston Consulting Group, 1974.

COMTE-SPONVILLE, André, *Le capitalisme est-il moral? Sur quelques ridicules et tyrannies de notre temps*, Albin Michel, Paris, 2009.

—, *Petit traité de grands vertus*, Points Seuil, Paris, 2006.

DOUGLAS, Roger, *Unfinished Business*, Random House, New Zealand, 1993.

HAYEK, Friedrich, *Law, Legislation and Liberty*, Routledge, 1982.

NOWAK, Maria, *L'espoir économique. De la microfinance à l'entrepreunariat social : les ferments d'un monde nouveau*, Jean-Claude Lattès, Paris, 2010.

PEYREFITTE, Alain, *Du "miracle" en économie. Leçons au Collège de France*, Odile Jacob, Paris, 1995.

—, *La Société de confiance. Essais sur les origines et la nature du développement*, Odile Jacob, Paris, 2005.

PRAHALAD, C.K., *The Fortune at the Bottom of the Pyramid: Eradicating Poverty Through Profits*, Wharton School Publishing, Wharton, 2009.

DE SOTO, Hernando, *The Mystery of Capital. Why Capitalism Triumphs in the West and Fails Everywhere Else*, Basic Books, New York, 2000.

YEW, Lee Kuan, *From Third World to First: The Singapore Story, 1965 – 2000*, Harper, New York, 2000.

GLOSSARY

BUSINESS MODEL: An expression describing how a business is organized to best serve the market. For example, press organizations can use a print business model or an online business model.

CAC 40: The name given to top 40 privately owned French companies listed on the stock exchange.

DUE DILIGENCE: An operation that consists in looking into a company's turnover, costs, profit and loss statements, contracts, commitments and legal proceedings as part of purchase or joint venture negotiations.

FREE CASH FLOW: What is left of a company's annual cash flow after capital expenditure. These flows can be positive, negative or zero. Positive cash flows generate dividends for shareholders, and negative cash flows mean shareholders must pay money into the company.

GDP (GROSS DOMESTIC PRODUCT): The sum of value-added by public and private sectors within a given country.

HEDGE FUNDS: Hedge funds are investment funds that use advanced investment strategies to earn returns for sophisticated investors such as wealthy individuals, banks or insurance companies. The word "hedge" implies that these funds take no risks, but this is not the case. Because they are unregulated, there are many different kinds of hedge funds.

JOINT VENTURE: This expression refers to companies that have split their capital between two groups. They are like daughter companies or marriages.

LMBO (LEVERAGED MANAGEMENT BUYOUT): An operation where management contracts debt to buy a company from its former shareholders. The company's profits and the proceeds from the sales of unused assets are devoted to reimbursing the debt.

CAPITALIZATION: The stock market value of a company. The value of a company is a multiple of its net profits. Companies with mixed results and low growth earn low scores of around 5. Companies with stable performances and strong growth can earn scores of up to 25. The average CAC 40 score is 15.

PRICE EARNINGS RATIO: This measures the ratio between a company's value and its results. Experience shows that companies with the same long-term strategy have a constant price earnings ratio (see CAC 40).

PRIVATE EQUITY FUNDS: Investors who do not wish to buy shares on the stock exchange give their money to brokers who invest the money in unlisted companies. Some private equity funds have become large economic institutions that employ almost one million employees. Managers' salaries are calculated by taking a fixed percentage of investments and adding bonuses based on profits made when the fund sells the companies it invests in.

RESEARCH & DEVELOPMENT (R&D): The name given to research and development activities leading to new products and prototypes that are tested before production.

REENGINEERING: An operation that consists in analyzing the operations of a company, division or department to identify more efficient workflows and processes. Today, new technologies and products are constantly being developed. These operations are therefore beneficial for companies when they are carried out every five to ten years.

SBF 120: The name given to the top 120 privately owned French companies listed on the stock exchange.

TEXTILE AND OPTICS, SEMI-FINISHED LENSES AND LABORATORIES: The textile and optical industries are both similar in the extreme variety of their production. The textile industry dealt with this variation by creating a two-tiered production system: textiles are produced in large fabric factories, and clothes are produced using this fabric in clothing factories.

The ophthalmic optics industry obeys the same principles. No eyes are alike, and to have perfect vision, you must visit an ophthalmologist who measures both eyes carefully. As around 60% of people need glasses, the global population theoretically needs around 7 to 8 billion different lenses.

The ophthalmic industry works along the same lines as the textile industry: large factories produce ready-to-wear and semi-finished lenses (the equivalent of fabric). Another kind of factory, called a prescription laboratory, transforms semi-finished lenses in line with orders from opticians. In the ophthalmic optics industry, there are companies that specialize in both areas (like Essilor and Hoya), companies that have specialized in semi-finished lenses (like Sola), and companies that specialize in laboratory professions and buy semi-finished lenses.

TABLES AND GRAPHS

Someone from far away standing in line

De : Jayanth B [jayanthb@essilorindia.com]
Envoyé : jeudi 16 décembre 2004 08:34
A: Alain Petard; Patrick Cherrier; FONTANET Xavier, DARNAULT Claude, ALFROID Philippe: VIDAL Henri
Objet : Photos
Pièces jointes : 08.Jpg; 07.jpg, 06.jpg, 05.jpg

Very interesting. Photograph of the first patient. She has insisted on paying too. Gives us some idea About the profile of the rural customer.
Best regards.
Jayanth

---- **Original Message** ---
From : Dr. S. Aravind
To : jayanthb@essilorindia.com
Cc: saugata@essilorindia.com
Sent : Friday, December 17, 2004 12:39 AM
Subject : FW: Photos

She insisted on paying herself.
Aravind

T 1

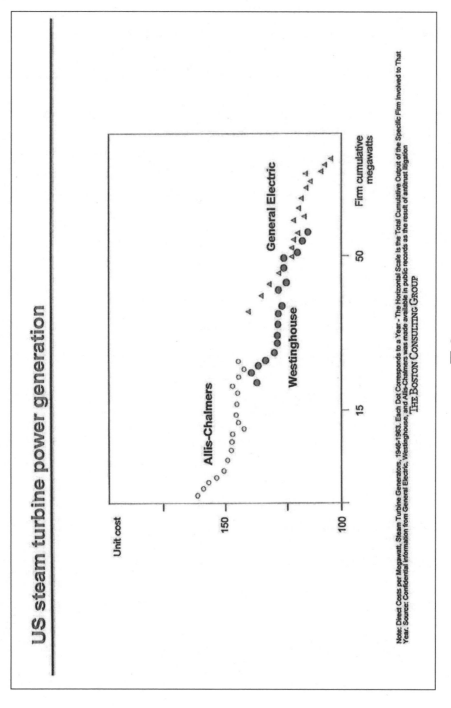

US steam turbine power generation

Unit cost

150

100

Allis-Chalmers

Westinghouse

General Electric

Firm cumulative
megawatts

15

50

Note: Direct Costs per Megawatt, Steam Turbine Generators, 1946-1963. Each Dot Corresponds to a Year - The Horizontal Scale is the Total Cumulative Output of the Specific Firm Involved to That Year. Source: Confidential information from General Electric, Westinghouse, and Allis-Chalmers was made available in public records as the result of antitrust litigation

THE BOSTON CONSULTING GROUP

T 2

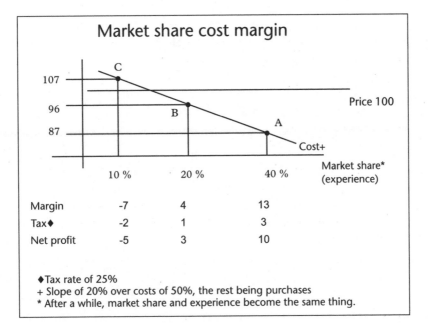

Market share cost margin

	10 %	20 %	40 %
Margin	-7	4	13
Tax♦	-2	1	3
Net profit	-5	3	10

♦Tax rate of 25%
+ Slope of 20% over costs of 50%, the rest being purchases
* After a while, market share and experience become the same thing.

T 3

The effect of dividends on growth

Sales	100	100	100
Assets*	100	100	100
Costs	75	75	75
Margin	25	25	25
Taxes	10	10	10
Net profit	15	15	15
Dividend	-	7,5	15
Reinvestment	15	7,5	-
Growth (%)	15	7,5	0

* Example of a heavy industry with an asset turnover of 1
Assets are the investments required to generate turnover of 100

T 4

Dividends and growth

	A	B	C
Net profit	10	3	-5
Dividend	7	-	-8
Reinvestment	3	3	3
Assets	50	50	50
Growth (%)	6	6	6

* This example is of a light industry with an asset turnover of 2

T 5

1976	Jeanneau	Beneteau
Sales	79	31
Assets*	41	14
Margin	12.2	5.5
Taxes	4.3	1.9
Net profit	7.9	3.6
Dividend	4.7	-
Debt	-	3.6
Investment	3.2	7.2
Sustainable growth	8 %	50 %
	(3.2/41)	(7.2/14)

T 6

EXTRACTS

Jean Jaurès

Article published in the Dépêche de Toulouse on 28 May 1890[1]

Ruling classes are always courageous. Throughout history, the ruling classes have been characterized by courage and voluntary risk-taking. He who rules risks what those who follow do not want to risk. He who accomplishes difficult or dangerous actions is respected by others. He who provides security for others at the risk of his own safety is a leader.

Courage, for the entrepreneur, is the spirit of enterprise and the refusal to depend on the State; for technicians, it is the refusal to make compromises on quality; for personnel or factory directors, it is defending the company; and, in the company, it is defending authority and, at the same time, discipline and order.

In medium-sized industries, there are many business owners who are, to a great extent, their own cashiers, their own accountants, their own draftsmen, their own foremen; they must deal with tiredness of the body, but also tiredness of the spirit that workers only feel fleetingly. They live in a world constantly at war, where solidarity does not exist. Until now, business owners have been unable to work together

---

1. Translated into English for the current work by Rhonda Campbell.

to protect themselves, where this is possible, from the failures that can destroy in a day a manufacturer's fortune and credit.

Producers wage a merciless war against each other; in the battle for clients, they sell merchandise at the lowest possible prices during years of crisis, they even sell below cost price. They must accept payment terms that, for their purchasers, At the slightest setback, the vigilant banker requests payment within 24 hours.

When workers accuse business owners of being pleasure-seekers who want to make money in order to enjoy themselves, they misunderstand the spirit of employers. No doubt there are business owners that enjoy themselves, but what real business owners want is to win the battle. There are many who, in increasing their fortune, do not increase their enjoyments; and in any case that is not the first thing on their minds They are happy to say, when they have positive results, that their efforts were not wasted, that there is a palpable outcome, and that something came of all the risks, and their power of action increased.

No, in truth, business owners in today's society, are not to be envied. And men should not look at each other angrily or with covetousness, but with a kind of mutual pity, that could be the precursor of justice!

Abraham LINCOLN

Declaration to Congress in 1860

You cannot bring about prosperity by discouraging thrift.

You cannot strengthen the weak by weakening the strong

You cannot help the poor man by destroying the rich.

You cannot further the brotherhood of man by inciting class hatred.

You cannot build character and courage by taking away man's initiative and independence.

You cannot help small men by tearing down big men.

You cannot lift the wage earner by pulling down the wage payer.

You cannot keep out of trouble by spending more than your income.

You cannot establish security on borrowed money.

You cannot help men permanently by doing for them what they will not do for themselves.

Frédéric BASTIAT

Harmful remedies[2]

When our brother is suffering, we must help him.

But good intentions are not the same thing as good treatments. One can very charitably give a remedy that kills.

A poor worker was ill.

When the doctor arrived, he took the man's pulse, made him stick his tongue out and said, "Young man, you do not eat enough."

"I believe you," said the dying man, "yet I was treated by a very wise old doctor. He gave me three-quarters of a loaf of bread every night. It is true he took the whole loaf in the morning and kept a quarter for his fees. I told him to leave as the treatment did not heal me."

"My friend, that doctor was very ignorant. He did not see that your blood is depleted. We must solve this problem. I will inject new blood into your left arm taken from the right arm. As long as you pay no attention to the blood lost from your right arm or during the operation, you will find my treatment works wonders."

This is the situation we find ourselves in. The government has said to the people, "You don't have enough bread, I'll give you some. But as I don't make bread myself, I'll start by taking it from you, and, after satisfying my appetite, which isn't small, I'll let you earn the rest."

Or, "You don't earn high enough wages; pay me more taxes. I'll distribute some of it to my agents, and with the rest, I'll give you more work. " And if the people only have eyes for the bread they are given, and forget the bread taken away from them; if they only see the small salary their taxes earn them, and forget the big salary taken away from them, this problem will only grow larger.

---

2. Translated from the French for the present work by Rhonda Campbell.

Frédéric BASTIAT

Mutual-aid societies[3]

The mutual-aid societies must be free, must have certain well-defined prerogatives and be in complete control of their own funds. They must be allowed sufficient flexibility to adapt their regulations to fit local needs.

Suppose that the government interferes. It is easy to imagine the role it will assign itself. Its first concern will be to take over all funds on the pretext of centralizing them; and, in order to make this measure more palatable, it will promise to increase them out of resources taken from the taxpayer. [...] The first unjust act will be to force into the society, through taxation, citizens who have no right to share in the benefits. The second unjust act will be to propose, in the name of unity, of solidarity (call it what you will), that all associations be merged into one, subject to uniform regulations.

But, I ask, what will happen to the morality of the institution when its treasury is fed by taxes; when no one, except possibly some bureaucrat, finds it to his interest to defend the common fund; when every member, instead of making it his duty to prevent abuses, delights in encouraging them; when all mutual supervision has stopped, and malingering becomes merely a good trick played on the government? The government, to give it its just due, will be disposed to defend itself; but, no longer being able to count on private action, will have to resort to official action. It will appoint various agents, examiners, controllers, and inspectors. It will set up countless formalities as barriers between the workers' claims and his relief payments. In a word, an admirable institution will, from its very inception, be turned into a branch of the police force.

The state will perceive, first of all, the advantages to be gained from adding to the vast throng of its appointees, from multiplying the number of jobs at its disposal, from extending its patronage and

---

3. Bastiat, Frédéric. *Economic Harmonies*. George B. de Huszar, trans. and W. Hayden Boyers, ed., Foundation for Economic Education, Inc., Irvington-on-Hudson, NY, 1996.

electoral influence. It will not realize that, in arrogating to itself a new function, it has also placed upon itself a new, and, indeed, a frightening responsibility. For what must the immediate consequence be? The workers will no longer look upon their common treasury as property to be administered and maintained by themselves, with their own claims on it limited by the extent of its resources. Little by little they will become accustomed to considering unemployment benefits, not as something provided by the limited funds that they have accumulated by their own foresight, but as a debt that society owes them. They will never admit that society cannot pay and will never be satisfied with the benefits they receive. The state will constantly be obliged to ask for new additions to the budget. At this point, encountering opposition from the treasury officials, it will find itself in inextricable difficulties. Abuses will increase all the time, and the government will shrink, as it always does, from rectifying them until there comes the day of explosion. But when this happens, the government will discover that it has to reckon with a population that has lost the ability to act for itself, that looks to a cabinet minister or an official for everything, even its livelihood, a population whose thinking has become so warped as to have lost any notion of right, property, liberty, or justice.

ADIE: A REAL ENTREPRENEURIAL NETWORK

Adie is an organization that was set up twenty years ago by Maria Nowak. It is based on a simple but brilliant idea. Adie supports unemployed people in France who wish to set up their own business– thus helping them create their own job and become their own boss – by using microfinance, a financial instrument that did not exist at the time.

Twenty years on, Adie is still going strong (it grew over 20% in 2009). Maintaining such a high rate of growth over such an extended period of time indicates the organization has tapped into a lasting trend.

Each microenterprise is a miracle in itself. It is the work of a courageous individual who, facing difficult circumstances, decides to take things into their own hands by becoming an entrepreneur. Each company satisfies the needs of clients by developing local services that can sometimes be franchised.

If we look at Adie's long-term results to the end of 2010, the organization could be described as a network of 65,000 microenterprises employing around 100,000 people. Not only does Adie have an admirable message in terms of trusting in human nature, it also makes a major contribution to the French economy. If the organization keeps growing at its current rate, it will come to represent 5% of companies with less than five employees. It will also be the largest privately owned employer in France. This initiative is indicative of a real societal change.

The public sector should develop new tax regulations for this sector, which is characterized by an extremely high asset turnover (Adie has around 50 million euros or $69 million in outstanding debt). This is especially true given it saves the state money in grants and spending.

The recent boom in new companies being registered in France confirms Nowak's initiative. The French bank Crédit Agricole was set up 160 years ago as the result of a similar project (loaning money to farmers that no one else trusted) – today Credit Agricole has 200 000 employees, and has a net worth of 72 billions euros. This seems to indicate that Adie has a bright future...

Ce volume,
publié aux Éditions Les Belles Lettres
a été achevé d'imprimer
en octobre 2011
sur les presses
de la Nouvelle Imprimerie Laballery
58500 Clamecy

N° d'éditeur : 7315
N° d'imprimeur : 110155
Dépôt légal : novembre 2011

Imprimé en France